DAVENPORT'S
SOUTH CAROLINA WILLS
AND ESTATE PLANNING
LEGAL FORMS

DAVENPORT'S SOUTH CAROLINA WILLS AND ESTATE PLANNING LEGAL FORMS

written by attorneys
Alex Russell and Robert Maxwell

BOOK AND FORMS FREE AT
WWW.DAVENPORTPUBLISHING.COM

PUBLICATION DATA

(informal, library may use different data)

Names: Russell, Alex, 1972- author ; Maxwell, Robert, 1960- author

Title: Davenport's South Carolina Wills And Estate Planning Legal Forms

Other Titles: Davenport's Wills

Description: Davenport Publishing 2023

Suggested Identifiers: 9798376868959, LCCN 2021909030, 9798748423373

Subjects: LCSH: Wills--United States;
                    Wills--United States--Forms;
                    Estate Planning--United States;
                    Legal Forms

Classification: LFF KF755 .C55 2022 (or as library chooses)
                    DDC 346.73 Rus--dc23 (or as library chooses)

9 8 7 6 5 4 3 2 1 0 0 0 0 0 2 3

WARNING

THIS PUBLICATION IS NOT A SUBSTITUTE FOR LEGAL ADVICE. Publisher and authors say and warn this publication is not giving any legal, accounting, or other professional services or advice, which if wanted can be obtained by consulting in person an attorney or some other professional. **No attorney-client relationship or any relationship creating a duty or obligation is agreed to or created by the purchase or use of this publication or forms.**

CHAPTER	TABLE OF CONTENTS	PAGE NUMBER

CHAPTER 1
BOOK BASICS AND LIST OF FORMS

ESTATE PLANNING CONTROLS THINGS IF LATER ABSENT, SICK, OR DEAD

From Davenport Publishing and written by attorneys this book covers "Estate Planning", about doing legal documents to control health care, property, money, children, funeral, and more if later absent, sick, or dead.

SOUTH CAROLINA LAW APPLIES TO PEOPLE LIVING HERE OR RETURNING

This book is for South Carolina and due to different laws Estate Planning books and legal forms can't be safely used for other states. State law in this area applies if a person: a) resides here as their main home, or b) resided here and left with firm plans to return even if person rents a home elsewhere like some students, military, and workers. For health care forms people should do forms to match state a health facility is in.

BOOK IS SHORT, HAS FORMS TO QUICKLY SEE, AND USES EMPHASIS

This book by attorneys is short so may read rough but lets person read in day the basics of the subject. The book also has ready-to-use legal forms people can quickly see and use. For emphasis paragraph titles, underlining, and boxes are used. To save space some small words are skipped and end quotation marks put before punctuation. This book capitalizes some legal words like Will, Testator, and Agent but this is optional.

PEOPLE CAN IN A FEW WAYS GET FORMS TO FILL OUT

To get forms to use people can 1) photocopy pages from book, 2) tear or cut out pages from book, or 3) at www.davenportpublishing.com get computer files to print (PDF is best option to avoid format changes). Usually legal forms use blank spaces to show where to add in words, like "I give _____ to _____". It is often fine to leave blank spaces in forms unfilled.

LEGAL SYSTEM IN ESTATE PLANNING ASKS WHAT DID PERSON WANT DONE

People have a legal right to control their health care, property, money, and family issues, and so judges, doctors, and others mostly just ask: **"Based on what a person wrote what did they likely want done?"** Neatness or nice wording is not needed. This book does cover requirements certain documents do have.

FORMS ARE BINDING LEGAL DOCUMENTS AND DO SIMPLE THINGS WELL

Estate Planning research shows a shocking 60% of people die without doing anything, 19% use a lawyer, and 21% use legal forms. Legal forms are good at most things involved in Estate Planning and make binding legal documents that judges, doctors, families, banks, and others must follow.

BOOK PROVIDES SOUTH CAROLINA "STANDARD FORM" OR SUITABLE FORM

Often a South Carolina agency, hospital, or the legislature has made a form that most people in the state use and call the "standard form", and doctors, judges, and others may not like to follow a different form. This book does provide the standard state form in area if it exists and in other areas a suitable form is provided. A form put into state law by the legislature to be used if wanted is called a "statutory form".

ESTATE PLANNING MOSTLY IS DOING SIMPLE THINGS IN 3 AREAS

Estate Planning is mostly doing simple things in 3 areas: After Death, Health Care, and Giving Power. Legal forms can be used to make binding legal documents in these areas. Many people just use 1 or 2 legal forms for Estate Planning, like many people do 1 Will and 1 health care form, but some do more.

THERE ARE 9 LEGAL FORMS FOR SOUTH CAROLINA IN THIS BOOK

AFTER DEATH FORMS

Form 1. Will (Standard) – a Will (also called a "Last Will And Testament") lets a person control things after their death like who gets their money and property, who is Executor handling things, and letting some easier legal options be used later to reduce costs and delays.

Form 2. Will (Guardians) – Will with parts added to name someone as Guardian to care for minor child under 18 if needed (like if no parent is available), and also name someone as Conservator to if needed manage money and property of a child and spend this on them till child reaches age 18.

Form 3. Self-Proving Affidavit – form often done with Will to later help prove it was properly signed.

Form 4. Tangible Personal Property List – lets person easily outside Will write more gifts to occur after death of "tangible personal property" like furniture, jewelry, vehicles, art, electronics, tools, and clothes.

HEALTH CARE FORMS

Form 5. Health Care Power Of Attorney – lets person name someone as Health Care Agent to control health care if they're incapacitated later, write health care instructions, and maybe do serious step of saying later stop health care if they're incapacitated and bad health likely won't improve (next form also does this).

Form 6. Declaration Of A Desire For A Natural Death – does serious act of saying stop care if later doctors think person is incapacitated and bad health won't improve with more care (this is a "Living Will").

Form 7. Do Not Resuscitate Order – does serious act of saying immediately from now on do not try certain health care, and this actually is 2 forms either a "D.N.R." form about "resuscitation" and not trying to help breathing or heart, or a "P.O.S.T." form about not trying many medical treatments listed in the form.

GIVING POWER FORMS

Form 8. Durable Power Of Attorney – lets power over money, property, and more be given during life to trusted person so they have legal power to help do things, like handle paying bills, and this book's form also has option for a parent to give power over a minor child under 18.

Form 9. Final Wishes – lets instructions be given and/or person named to control issues with body after death like funeral, cremation, and burial (without this form closest family by law usually handles all this).

BOOK COVERS LAW MOST PEOPLE WANT AND SOME STATE DIFFERENCES

This book covers what most people want to know about Estate Planning. State laws are fairly similar across the U.S. and this book covers the main legal ideas. The book also covers some ways South Carolina law is different. After reading this book some people may want to do more legal research or see a lawyer.

THIS BOOK SHOULD SUIT PEOPLE WITHOUT STRANGE SITUATIONS OR WISHES

This book and its forms can't cover every issue that matters to everyone but it should suit people without strange situations or wishes about Estate Planning, which is probably most people like maybe over 90%. Strange situations or wishes that may need more research or a lawyer include: a) unusual wishes for gifts, b) wealth over $3 million, c) big medical concerns in family, d) property or money going to person with disability or "special needs", or e) wish to hide or move assets to quickly qualify for government programs. Many people re-do Estate Planning forms including their Will about each decade as their lives change.

ESTATE PLANNING OFTEN IS NOT VITAL

Despite what people may be told Estate Planning is usually not vital and worth much time or money. It usually does not: cut taxes unless person is a multi-millionaire, create new wealth, cut legal costs much, cut delay much, affect health care unless a person is suddenly incapacitated and rush decision needed, or affect children since a parent dying is rare and if needed a judge and family can do needed things. For young adults or parents the benefits of costly Estate Planning seem low since only about 9% of people die before 60, and only 0.2% of children under 19 had 2 parents die to probably ever need a Guardian. See _Social Security Census Tables by Felicitie Bell_; _Life Factors & Mortality Study, Census Study 288_.

INSURANCE MAY HELP MORE THAN COSTLY ESTATE PLANNING BY LAWYER

Instead of forms a lawyer can be paid to write complex Estate Planning documents but they can cost $1000s, take months, and make mistakes. In life people weigh costs and benefits and risks and often go with lower cost option. If people want to spend money in this area they can buy term life insurance of $100,000 via questionnaire but no exam ("simplified issue") for $50+ a month or $400+ yearly from MetLife, State Farm, Haven, Ladder, SBLI, or AIG. Doing nothing and just saving money also can help family.

SOME LESS COMMON AND LESS USEFUL FORMS ARE NOT IN BOOK

This book skips less common or less useful documents. A "Codicil" can modify a Will but it is easier and safer to just re-do Will. Some people do "Revocable Living Trust" so Trust entity with Trustee holds property or money during a person's life, done to after death avoid small delay, costs, or work (by "avoiding probate"). This is rare as it requires immediately moving 100% of person's things into a Trust with maybe years of costs and hassle, mostly for small benefits for people who are probably happy to do work to get things by Will. Next, "Childrens Trust" papers can be done so Trust upon a death gets a minor child's money or property to manage until 18, but this is uncommon due to possible years of hassle and costs and (as this book shows) since it rarely matters and most Wills already arrange Guardian, Conservator, and Custodian to help a child. Some people do a "Pet Trust" to give money for pet, but it's easier in Will to give money to person given pet. Complex documents may be suggested for tax reasons, but as this book explains there are usually no taxes.

CHAPTER 2
TERMS, PROPERTY, AND HELPFUL INFORMATION FORM

THERE ARE BASIC TERMS AND IDEAS IN ESTATE PLANNING

Some legal terms and ideas are basic to Estate Planning.

■ "Estate Planning" is person doing legal documents to control things if they are later absent, sick, or dead. After a document is done a person is still free to sell or transfer property, instruct doctors, or change forms.

■ A "person doing a legal document" and "doing a form" means the form is for and affects that person.

■ A "Will" or "will" (this book uses upper case "W") is a legal document done to control issues after death. The phrase "Last Will And Testament" is used since a "Testament" long ago was a small document done along with a Will to do some things. If no Will is done a person is described as being "intestate".

■ A person who died is called "decedent" or "deceased". A person getting a Will gift is called "recipient", "beneficiary", or "heir" if related (they "inherit"). "Survive" or "surviving" is to be alive after someone died.

■ A person named to do things after someone's death is called by most people and this book "Executor", but in official papers and Wills the term "Personal Representative" is officially now used in South Carolina.

■ A person doing a Will is called "Testator" or "Will maker". Before about 1990 a woman Testator was called a "Testatrix" and woman Executor called an "Executrix" but this is no longer often done.

■ "Probate" is a legal process to do things after death like transfer property, authorize a Guardian, and handle creditors. Due to nice changes in law probate is now often "informal", faster, and less expensive.

■ "Property" is either: 1) "real property" which is land and buildings ("real estate"), 2) "personal property" which is things not real property, like cash, accounts, stocks, tools, clothes, cars, jewelry, and art, or 3) "fixtures" which are things tied to real property (like fences, posts, lighting, and wired-in appliances).

■ Legal documents to control health care things are often called "Health Care Directives", but names vary.

■ Forms giving power are often named "Power of Attorney" forms, where a person called the "Principal" gives power to someone called the "Attorney-in-Fact" or "Agent".

■ State law is the Code of Laws of South Carolina, which is made up of statutes or sections. A reference to a state law can look like, for example, "S.C. Code §1-2-345" with "§" or "s" meaning statute or section. A form found in state law to use if people want is a "statutory form".

4

LEGAL DOCUMENTS MAY NEED TO BE "WITNESSED" OR "NOTARIZED"

Legal documents to be valid may need to be "witnessed", which is someone acting as witness watching person doing form sign and then witness signs. Documents may need to be "notarized", which is person who is a "notary" (also called "notary public") see signing and use ink stamp on page and then notary sign too. This book explains for each form if witnesses or a notary is needed and also says who can be a witness. Notaries are found at some banks, brokers, insurance agents, courts, and government offices but they might be busy or they might only help existing customers. A helpful notary often can be found using a phonebook.

ANYONE CAN FILL IN MOST OF FORM, AND LATER TRY TO KEEP ORIGINAL

When filling out a form except for signatures other parts can be filled in by a person not doing document, maybe because of a person's good handwriting or typing. After a legal form is done usually a person tries to keep the original and only hand out copies but situations vary. Some people do "multiple originals" by having everyone sign identical documents to have many pages with real ink signatures, but this can be confusing.

"ESTATE" MEANS PROPERTY OF DECEDENT OR ENTITY HOLDING ITEMS

The "Estate" or "probate estate" is all property and money of a dead person that on death did not somehow automatically transfer to other owners. "Estate" is also the word for the temporary entity run by Executor to do things after a death (sort of like a small corporation). A dead person's money and accounts might be renamed or moved to a bank account under an Estate name, like "Estate of John Eric Smith".

PROBABLY DO NEW FORMS IF DIVORCE, MARRY, HAVE CHILD, OR MOVE

Divorcing, marrying, having a new child, or moving to a new state can have big legal effects. If any of these events occur it is recommended people do a new Will and other Estate Planning papers soon. To help most states say a Will from another state is still valid but this is not always certain.

"INTESTATE" LAW SAYS WHERE THINGS GO AT DEATH IF THERE IS NO WILL

State "intestate law" says where property and money goes if no valid Will was done before person died (except for certain rights of spouses, family, and creditors). Intestate law often say half and sometimes all goes to any surviving spouse (if any), then half or any remainder goes to decedent's children natural or adopted (or if dead their child gets that share), then next closest family, then other family, and then the state. Many people are happy with intestate law and intentionally die with no Will, but many people prefer a Will.

PERSON CAN ONLY GIFT IN WILL WHAT THEY OWN AT DEATH

A person can only gift by Will things they own at death so people should research what they own. Basically by law a person usually owns all they earn as wages and salary, owns their share of income and profit tied to property they own, and owns or partly owns any things their money buys or improves. But married people in Community Property law states mostly face different rules about sharing ownership. And for property with "title" documents (real estate or vehicles) or where there is a "listed owner" (like accounts) the named persons are usually the legal owners unless evidence shows special circumstances. Note, a person during life can sell property, make gifts, or transfer things even if items are named in a Will, so people should consider if they already sold or gave away property they also name in a Will gift.

THINGS OWNED IN SPECIAL WAYS MAY LIMIT WILL GIFTING

A person should consider if they own real estate or other property in special ways which may limit gifting by Will. Laws in different states vary but some special joint ways are:

    a) "joint tenant with right of survivorship" or similar so then property transfers automatically to the other named owners regardless of a Will, which in some states is often how a family house is held,

    b) a "life estate" where papers say if life of someone ends the other people in papers get item, and

    c) "Trust property" if paperwork made a Trust entity and property was actually transferred into it, so then the Trust papers control where things put in the Trust go on someone's death.

But normal joint property for the part owned <u>can</u> be gifted by Will, like "I give the half of Boat that I own with Aunt Jo to Ed Fox". Joint ownership can occur many ways like if people do joint papers, agree to own jointly, buy with joint funds, or a gift was to multiple persons.

WARNING: "NON-PROBATE PROPERTY" TRANSFERS IGNORE ANY WILL

Money or property that for some reason automatically transfers on death to other owners is called "non-probate property", and such things quickly transfer as arranged even if a Will names the same items. Examples of non-probate property are: a) a "designated beneficiary" form done earlier names person to get account or investment, b) transfer-on-death account, and c) real estate like a house held by 2 people as "joint tenants with survivorship" or similar ways so survivor gets things. Property and money in a Trust also ignores a Will and transfers as trust papers say. Insurance with a beneficiary usually ignores a Will. Trying to do non-probate transfers <u>for all things</u> is called "avoiding probate", but it is rare as it may make living and paperwork a hassle for years, benefits are small, and it is hard to not miss an item and fail. <u>When doing a Will a person should consider non-probate transfers that will occur automatically on death and consider what property and money will be left to transfer by Will.</u>

NO FEDERAL, SOUTH CAROLINA, OR OTHER TAX IS OWED AT A DEATH

Usually no tax is owed as a result of a death, including no estate, inheritance, death, or similar taxes. This is because the "Federal Estate And Gift Tax" only starts when tax credit is used up covering <u>$12.92 million per person in 2023</u> (with yearly rises for inflation). South Carolina ended its Estate Tax in 2005 and has no other taxes that might be owed upon a death. Property located in a different state might face tax upon a death but most states have no such taxes or exempt at least the first $3 million in value. <u>Usually only multi-millionaires in South Carolina need to worry about taxes being owed due to a death.</u>

SOME PEOPLE DO "HELPFUL INFORMATION" FORM

It is <u>not a real legal form that legally does anything but a person can do a "Helpful Information" form</u> so family or friends after person's death have more information about property, money, debts, and other things. Neatness is not needed and often person does it quickly, writes in more over time, and prints and attaches pages with info. The form is often kept with a Will and at death goes to Executor or family. <u>See next pages.</u>

ESTATE PLANNING HELPFUL INFORMATION

Give information to help family, friends, and Executor after your death. If needed attach more forms or blank pages.

1. Personal Information (Name, Birthdate, Social Security #, special family details, other):

2. Real estate, vehicles, and other tangible property of high value (especially if people may not find them):

3. Non-tangible assets like stocks, accounts, investments, loans owed you, and businesses of high value:

4. Possible income or insurance of high value like pensions, retirement, disability, insurance, or contracts:

5. Debts owed by you like credit card, loan, student loan, mortgage, vehicle loan, and accounts payable:

6. Names and contact information of professionals used (attorneys, accountants, brokers, doctors, others):

7. Computer passwords and helpful files, document places, and safes or safe-deposit boxes codes/keys:

8. Other helpful things, wishes for funeral, special requests, and any last messages to family and friends:

CHAPTER 3
WILL BASICS

WILL LETS "TESTATOR" CONTROL THINGS AFTER DEATH

A Will is done by a person called "Testator" or "Will Maker" to control some things after their death. Testator <u>when signing</u> must be at least 18 years old, of sound mind (rational with sufficient memory), and not be under duress (unfair pressure or threat). Rarely is a person not mentally fit enough to do a Will.

SIGN WILL IN FRONT OF 2 WITNESSES WHO THEN SIGN

WILL TO BE VALID MUST BE WRITTEN AND SIGNED WITH 2 WITNESSES

To be a valid Will in South Carolina it must a) show it is meant as a Will, b) be written, and c) be signed in front of 2 witnesses who sign too. A Will must be put on paper and a "Video Will", "Audio Will", or online or computer Will is powerless. Verbal promises about things after death are mostly invalid if not in a Will. Some states but <u>not</u> South Carolina let 2 witnesses be skipped if a Will is all handwritten by person doing it.

WITNESS MUST BE AT LEAST 18

<u>The 2 persons acting as witnesses must be at least age 18</u>. It is slightly preferable they not be very old or living far away. Almost anyone can act as witness in South Carolina to properly complete a Will. <u>But unless there is 2 other witnesses then any gifts to a witness, their spouse, or their children are limited</u> to what they'd get by "intestate law" which applies if no Will was done. Due to this problem most lawyers try to use "disinterested" witnesses who aren't themselves, their spouse, or their children named in any Will gift. Though not required most lawyers also try to not use as witness a person who is named in Will as Executor, Guardian, Conservator, or similar. Often used as witness is friend, stranger, some employee, or family.

TESTATOR AND 2 WITNESSES SIGN A WILL WHEN ALL TOGETHER

To complete a Will the Testator signs and then usually 2 witnesses sign often within a few minutes. Everyone should be in 1 room and see hand of each person sign. Witnesses before signing quietly read the 1 paragraph they sign and not whole Will. Testator need not initial Will pages. Witnesses showing ID is not required but usual. Testator or witness need not use their full legal name if they dislike it and rarely used it.

TESTATOR NEED NOT SAY ANYTHING WHEN SIGNING

<u>Testator when signing Will need not say anything</u>. Some states but <u>not</u> South Carolina require Testator say aloud it is their Will, which lawyers call "publishing" it. As an option some people do choose to say a thing like, "My name is ____ and this is the Will I want and do voluntarily and I want you 2 people to witness". Some Testators also chat with witnesses a few minutes to help show they know what they're doing.

KEEP SIGNED WILL IN SAFE PLACE IT CAN BE FOUND AFTER A DEATH

People should keep Will so it can be found within days of a death, like in desk, drawer, safe, or less often a safe deposit box at bank. A Will can be given to a person to hold. It may help to tell people where to find Will and any key. In South Carolina a Will while a person is alive may <u>not</u> be filed at a court for safekeeping.

CANCELING OLD WILLS IS USUALLY NOT A PROBLEM

So a new Will is followed old Wills should be canceled ("revoked") but this is easy and rarely a problem. A new Will can say old Wills are revoked to cancel them, and most do this including Will forms in this book. Also to revoke Will a person can write "void" or "cancelled" or "X" on a Will, preferably with a witness to this. But crossing out just part of a Will often has no effect. Revoking a Will doesn't bring back an earlier Will.

MOST WILLS SAY USE LESS COSTLY AND SHORTER "INFORMAL" PROBATE

To help most Wills say use "informal probate" which is a legal option to reduce some costs and delays. Usually probate after a death is not too costly or slow, and often over 95% of value gets to wanted persons.

MOST WILLS SAY TO SKIP COSTLY BOND

Most Wills helpfully say no "bond" or "surety" is required for any Executor, Guardian, or Conservator. This is insurance bought from an insurance company to insure against misconduct. But the person writing a Will usually does not want this since any person named is trusted and insurance cost uses up estate assets.

MOST WILLS HAVE "MISCELLANEOUS" PART WITH HELPFUL LANGUAGE

Most Wills have "Miscellaneous" part with paragraphs of legal language to avoid some legal problems.

WILL NAMES AN EXECUTOR TO DO THINGS AFTER A DEATH

WILL NAMES "EXECUTOR" TO ACT AND HAVE POWER AFTER A DEATH

Often a Will names someone as "Executor" to act after a death like carry out gifts, handle debts, and do probate. The law gives Executors many powers and rights to do things, like collect and move money and property to new owners. If a Will does not name a person a judge can pick someone, but close family may argue about who to pick. Naming 2 people to both do this job is possible but rare due to risk of arguments and delay, and since any 1 person named should be trusted. The person named Executor can get Will gifts.

"PERSONAL REPRESENTATIVE" IS NEW NAME FOR EXECUTOR

In South Carolina the term "Personal Representative" is now used in Wills and official legal papers for person handling things after a death, but most people and this book still mostly use the old term Executor.

EXECUTOR CAN BE PAID, AND ESTATE PAYS FOR ALL THINGS

Many states let Executor ask for pay for hours worked or percent like 2% of value of all things handled, which is fairly small and fair. Pay is often not asked for to avoid income tax to Executor and leave more for Will gifts. Money an Executor needs like for attorneys, fees, repairs, and more comes from estate assets.

EXECUTOR IS PERSON AT LEAST 18, AND SECOND PERSON RARELY NEEDED

A person to be Executor must be 18 or older. They needn't be a state resident or even U.S. citizen but being local makes their later work easier. A judge later may not let someone they think is unsuitable serve as Executor especially if it involves past crimes. A judge can remove a person doing a bad job as Executor. Some Wills name a 2nd person to serve if a first person is unavailable, but most people skip this since it's rarely needed, if seen a new Will can be done, or if needed a judge can pick someone. But if people want to add 2nd person words can be added, like: "or if they are reasonably unable to serve I name ____ to serve".

CHAPTER 4
WILL GIFTS INCLUDING RESIDUE

MAIN USE OF WILL IS TO SAY GIFTS TO HAPPEN AFTER DEATH

Most people use Will to say what happens to their property and money after their death, usually by making various gifts in the Will. Verbal and even most written statements about this are not usually valid outside a Will. A Will can control property acquired after it was signed. Note, some families if all agree may informally hand out small items in way decedent mentioned they wanted to gift, but this is not fully proper.

GIFTING IN WILL USING SIMPLE WORDS OFTEN IS BEST

Making gifts in a Will using simple words is often best, using words like "I give to" and "I gift to". This is legally fine and avoids confusing legal words like "bequest", "devise", and "legacy" which few people know.

PERSON IS MOSTLY FREE TO GIFT THEIR THINGS AS WANTED

People are mostly free to give at death their money and property as they want, like give a child nothing, give all to a charity, or give all to a friend. But a spouse may have some rights which this book covers later.

IN WILL CAN DO "SPECIFIC GIFTS" TO GIFT PARTICULAR PROPERTY

Most Wills have "specific gifts" to gift particular things. Specific gifts can be any property, like "I give boat to Ed Blom" and "I give UBank account #84553873 to Sue Wu". If a gift is not clear the law assumes all of a kind of thing is given, like "I give jewelry to Ann Po" means all jewelry. But gifting specific property can have surprises like value of an item can change or a Will gift may fail to occur since property is no longer owned.

IN WILL CAN DO "GENERAL GIFTS" LIKE OF MONEY

Wills can do "general gifts" where what is gifted is not particular property but can be flexibly chosen, like "I give 1 of my 3 cars to Ed Po" which lets an Executor pick which car. The usual general gift is money, like "I give $5 to Ed Vu". Money gifts are easy to write, let equal gifts be made, and are safer since specific items might not be owned at death. To carry out money gifts an Executor uses accounts or sells some property.

"RESIDUE CLAUSE" IS CATCH-ALL THAT HELPFULLY GIFTS ANYTHING LEFT

Most Wills by their end have a Residue Clause to gift property or money not gifted or used in Will or other way, sometimes called a "catch-all" or "left-over" clause. The Residue Clause is covered later in this Chapter.

SOUTH CAROLINA ALLOWS "GIFT LISTS" TO BE DONE TO MAKE SOME GIFTS

This book later shows how South Carolina lets "Gift Lists" give tangible personal property outside a Will.

PERSON IN WILL GIFT USUALLY MUST SURVIVE OR GIFT DOES NOT OCCUR

Many Wills like this book's Will forms say person named in Will gift must survive (live past) Testator for the gift to occur unless gift language specifically says different. If survival is not clearly required for a Will gift what then occurs if a named recipient is dead can be unclear (like due to confusing state "anti-lapse" laws). People doing a Will should consider how Will gifts to people dying before Testator usually have no effect. Many people if they see person in Will gift has died re-do Will or just trust the Residue Clause to handle it.

SOME PEOPLE ADD "ALTERNATE BENEFICIARY" MAYBE FOR SPECIAL ITEMS

A person named in a Will gift dying before a Testator is rare, and if seen most people just re-do Will to add new person or let Residue Clause handle it. But some people to prepare for this rare event maybe for special items write in an alternate beneficiary, like "I give Boat to Ed Wu but if they don't survive me to Ben Fox".

WILL CAN SAY IF RECIPIENT DIES A GIFT GOES TO "LINEAL DESCENDANTS"

A Will gift can say it goes to person but if they don't survive then to their "lineal descendants per stirpes". Descendants are a person's children and grandchildren. "Per stirpes" is about "how" to spread things and means "by root" or "by branch", and basically tries to divide things so each family branch gets equal share. A family branch that died off with no one left is ignored. Most Wills use "lineal descendants" language in a Residue Clause and it also can be put in other gifts if wanted. An example shows how it works:

A Will may say **"Furniture to Sue Wu but if they don't survive to lineal descendants per stirpes"**, and this means if Sue Wu died and her son Ken Wu is living and her son Ben Wu has died but left 2 children then legally under the law Ken Wu gets 50% and Ben Wu's 2 children each get 25%.

PROPERTY OR MONEY IN A JOINT GIFT GOES TO MULTIPLE PEOPLE

The same property or money in a "joint gift" can go to multiple people to each get a part interest, like "I give boat and all hats to Ann Wu and Sue Han" means each person owns 50% of every item. People later can split things by agreement or as Executor suggests, or Executor can sell items and split the money. If a person in a joint gift has died their part of things usually is left to transfer under the Residue Clause.

GIFT BENEFICIARIES CAN GET PERCENTAGE RATHER THAN EQUAL SHARE

If a Will gift goes to many people the law assumes equal shares, but if wanted percentages can be put to make unequal gifts, like "I give boat 90% to Ed Wu and 10% to Joe Hud".

CONDITIONS ON WILL GIFTS ARE RARE DUE TO POSSIBLE PROBLEMS

Putting conditions on a gift, like "I give Ann Poe $90 if she graduates college", can cause problems like years of delay, risk of lawsuits, and big attorneys fees, and due to this conditions are rarely put on Will gifts.

HELPFUL LAWS OFTEN REQUIRE PERSON SURVIVE 120 HOURS TO GET GIFT

Laws in most states say a person dying within 120 hours of someone is seen as having died earlier so often a Will gift to them is ignored. This avoids legal problems like need to know time of death if people die near each other, and avoids an item going to someone who quickly dies so item must be transferred again.

LATER DIVORCE OR MURDER CANCELS WILL GIFTS

South Carolina law says person divorcing or murdering Testator usually cancels all Will gifts to person.

CAN LEAVE SOME WILL GIFT LINES BLANK OR WRITE THINGS LIKE "SKIPPED"

A person writing a Will can choose to not use some gifts lines in a Will legal form, like by just leaving them blank, writing things like "SKIPPED" or "NONE" in them, or using a computer to delete some gift lines. Judges and others usually do not care about neatness or empty spaces in Wills.

12

THE "RESIDUE CLAUSE" IS CATCH-ALL THAT HELPS GIFT ANYTHING LEFT

Wills by their end have a Residue Clause to gift property or money not gifted earlier in Will or used in other ways. All things that transfers this way is called the "Residue". Many people gift most their money and property this way as it skips need to describe things and has less legal risk. Later after a death after applying a Residue Clause if anything is left (which happens in rare cases) then closest "heirs" get things (this means closest family). The Residue can go to multiple people and to avoid an equal split percentages can be used.

USUAL RESIDUE CLAUSE HAS 2 PARTS

A short 2 part Residue Clause is usual and is used in this book's Wills, and it has:

1) 1st space to name 1 or more persons to get things if they survive Testator (many name a spouse or closest family here), and if several people are named but only some survive then survivors split things, and

2) 2nd space to name persons to get things if all in 1st space don't survive (so these are fallbacks) (many name next family or friends here), and if a person in 2nd space died their descendants get their share.

EXAMPLE OF 2 PART RESIDUE CLAUSE:

"RESIDUE CLAUSE: I give money and property not gifted earlier:

A) to _____ my husband John Paul Doe _____ if they survive me, then

B) to _____ Sam Doe my son, Beth Wu my daughter, and Greta Fisher my friend _____ and if any of those just named do not survive me their part goes to their lineal descendants, per stirpes."

In this example if John Paul Doe has survived then he gets things. But if John Paul Doe hasn't survived and also Sam Doe hasn't survived and he left 2 daughters, then those 2 daughters split the 1/3 share of Sam Doe so get 1/6 each and other 2 persons in second part Beth Wu and Greta Fisher get 1/3 each.

A FEW PEOPLE RE-WRITE RESIDUE CLAUSE TO HAVE 1 PART

A normal Residue Clause of 2 parts is often fine and basically person put in 1st part usually gets things. A small fraction of people may want to modify a Will to have a "1 Part Residue Clause" which gifts to a group more equally, and also says if anyone named here die their descendants like children get their part. People with no spouse and no children are likelier to do this change, but even they often don't bother and just use this book's Will forms as is. See Example below for exact words to use if people want this change.

EXAMPLE OF 1 PART RESIDUE CLAUSE:

"RESIDUE CLAUSE: The rest, residue, and remainder of my estate, property of any kind and nature, and anything I have an interest in, I give to _ Adam Doe and Beth Wu _ who survive me, and to lineal descendants per stirpes of any person just named who did not survive me."

In this example if Adam hasn't survived but had 2 children they each get 25%, and if Beth Wu survived she gets 50%. Or if Beth Wu also hadn't survived and had 5 kids they split her part and each gets 10%.

MUST SUFFICIENTLY DESCRIBE NAMES AND PROPERTY IN WILL GIFTS

WILL GIFT IS FINE IF PEOPLE CAN TELL WHAT TESTATOR LIKELY MEANT

The basic legal rule is <u>a Will gift is sufficiently detailed if people who knew Testator can inform Executor or a judge what Testator meant more likely than not</u>, and certainty is not needed to carry out a Will gift.

PUTTING NAMES OF PEOPLE OR GROUPS IN WILL GIFTS IS FAIRLY EASY

Names in Wills are easy. It is assumed people gift to persons they know so it's OK to use common short names unless 2 friends or family have same name. Details can be added if names may not be recognized or to be friendly, like "I give $5 to maid Ann Ax" and "I give $5 to my loyal funny pals Ed Po and Ann Vix". If people used a nickname "also known as" or "a/k/a" may help, like "I give $5 to Ed Wu a/k/a Old Fishy". Gifts can go to non-persons like a government, charity, or group if they're a real organization. Examples are: "I give $5 to The Salvation Army, "I give $5 to Horry County government, SC", "I give $5 to Ivy School, Boyd, SC", and "I give clothes to Calgary Church in Charleston, SC". <u>People often phone to ask for charity name</u>.

DESCRIPTIONS OF PROPERTY IN WILL GIFTS IS FAIRLY EASY

Describing items in gifts is easy since people rarely own similar items, so often fine is "I give ax to Ed Wu" and "I give oak table to Sue Po". It's OK to gift by category or list, like "I give tools to Ed Lee" and "I give ax, van, and cow to Ann Vix". Financial assets can use plain words, like "bank accounts" or "stocks", but some details can help, like "UBank account ending #1511". <u>Using item location in a Will gift is risky</u> as judges may ignore Will gifts if it seems items were placed to affect gifting and not "independently significant" life reason. So, "I give Ed Po items in safe and desk" a judge might ignore, but "I give Ed Wu hats at cabin" likely is OK.

DESCRIBING REAL PROPERTY IS HARD SO MANY USE RESIDUE OR TITLE

Using a "legal description" for Will gifts of real property (real estate) is legally best but hard to do <u>exactly</u> right as the law wants. This can look like: "Lot 3, Block 8 of Dale's Addition to City of Aiken according to plat in Cass Country Register of Deeds in Horry County", or thing like "north 10 feet of east 90 feet of Lot 6 of Northwest Parcel…". It is less legally safe but common to use plain words to give real property, like a house can be given by "I give 21 Ivy Rd., York, SC to John Paul Ax" or land by "I give land in Clay County, SC to David Eric Poe". A Will gift which just names a location <u>does</u> cover all land, buildings, and fixtures there. <u>But the legally safest way to gift real property is 1) do nothing specific so it's covered by Will Residue Clause which covers things not specifically gifted other ways, or 2) have lawyer or broker add names to the land title</u>.

SIMPLE WILL WITH MOST GIFTING DONE BY RESIDUE CLAUSE IS OFTEN BEST

Writing a simple Will without many gifts and much left blank and then using Residue Clause is often best.

If there <u>is a spouse</u> often people do a few small gifts to friends and other family, then use Residue Clause of Will to gift spouse the Residue, and then name a few fallback persons in the Residue Clause.

If there is <u>no spouse and no child</u> often people do a few small gifts, then gift family or friends the Residue.

<u>A parent with young children</u> if married to other parent often gifts Residue to them, and as fallback gifts the Residue to the children. Or if not married a parent mostly gifts to their children using the Residue Clause.

CHAPTER 5
DEBT, MARRIAGE, AND YOUNG CHILD ISSUES

DEBT, MARRIAGE, AND YOUNG CHILD CAN CAUSE ISSUES

This Chapter deals with debt issues, marriage issues, and young child issues. People can skip the parts of this Chapter they think won't matter to them.

DEBT ISSUES

PAYING DECEDENT'S DEBTS MAY USE UP RESOURCES AND REDUCE GIFTS

Creditors decedent owed can ask judge to be paid from decedent's money and property before Will gifts and other transfers are done. But if decedent had under about $40,000 of money and property plus a house creditors often don't bother, for reasons said below. Resources to pay debts first come from things in Will Residue, then Will general gifts like of money, then Will specific gifts, and then any non-probate transfers. Some debts like for probate, attorney, funeral, and health care have priority to be paid first. Helpfully spouse and family aren't usually personally liable to pay decedent's debts unless they guaranteed or co-signed. People should consider how paying debts may use up money or property, leaving less to carry out Will gifts.

BEFORE DEBTS ARE PAID MAY COME SOME FAMILY RIGHTS

Most states say surviving spouse and children can claim "family rights" before debts are paid, which lets family get something despite big debts. Many states give family 1) "living allowance" right to money to live on for 1-2 years, 2) "exempt property" right to often about $30,000 of decedent's property, and 3) "homestead" right explained later. Creditors know of family rights so often don't seek payment if told decedent left little. Often a person by Will gifts mostly to family like over 50% so they're happy and don't bother to claim family rights, but if family rights are used it may leave less to carry out Will gifts. People can research their state.

"HOMESTEAD" LAWS IN MANY STATES PROTECT HOME FOR FAMILY

"Homestead" laws in many states say decedent's creditors can't seek payment by foreclosing and then selling decedent's house if spouse or children under 18 are there (unless equity is big, like over $200,000). Homestead laws also often say spouse or minor children get ownership of decedent's house (or right to live there for their life in some states) if decedent owned it and despite a Will gift giving it to other people. South Carolina has little protection of a homestead but may give some tax benefits if a spouse receives it. Often people give house to family especially spouse by Will or putting them on title so they're happy so don't bother with these rights, but if rights are used it may interfere with Will gifts. People can research their state.

OFTEN SECURED DEBTS LIKE MORTGAGE OR VEHICLE LIEN AREN'T PAID OFF

Most states say secured debts like house mortgage or car lien are not paid off after death but remain even if Will says generally to pay debts. This book's Will forms clearly say don't pay secured debts unless person writes in Will to do so. This avoids using up much paying off debts so less is left to carry out Will gifts. If a Testator wants to pay off secured debts a) they can in Will also give enough cash to pay debt, or b) write an order to pay in Will (like "I order mortgage on cabin paid off"). Of course people who get Will gift of house or car with lien or mortgage must usually sell fast or pay monthly to avoid later foreclosure or repossession.

MARRIAGE ISSUES

MOST STATES USE "SEPARATE PROPERTY LAW" FOR SPOUSES

Most states including South Carolina use "Separate Property Law" system saying married people <u>mostly own all their money and property separately</u> and not jointly 50/50 with spouse. So a spouse <u>is</u> mostly free to sell during life or gift in Will their things. But joint ownership by 2 spouses can arise in ways (like by paying half a purchase price, agreement, a gift was to both spouses, or spouses do paperwork to own jointly).

"COMMUNITY PROPERTY" LAW APPLIES IN OTHER STATES FOR SPOUSES

There are 9 states mostly in West and South U.S.A. that use "Community Property" law for spouses (Arizona, California, Louisiana, Idaho, Nevada, New Mexico, Texas, Washington, and also Wisconsin). This says if a married person lives in these states <u>most property or money gotten is usually owned 50/50 by spouses as "Community Property"</u> if it relates to activities during a marriage (like from labor or wages, or active management of a small business) or if bought or improved with existing Community Property. Most people avoid these issues unless recently moving to or from these states.

"JOINT WILL" SIGNED BY BOTH SPOUSES IS NOT RECOMMENDED

Some couples sign 1 "Joint Will" or "Contract To Make A Will" done by lawyer which says spouses gives all to the other if they die first, then says last living spouse gives to all children equally, and usually says a spouse may not change this. This is not recommended, banned in some states, and few people do this.

SPOUSE CAN SEEK "ELECTIVE SHARE" OF THEIR DEAD SPOUSE'S THINGS

For fairness and so a surviving spouse has enough to live on, many states give a spouse if unhappy with what Will gifts them a right to choose (elect) an "Elective Share" of dead spouse's property and money. This avoids a spouse feeling to be safe they must divorce to get property or money rather than stay married. Some states set Elective Share based on years of marriage up to 50% after like 15 years. South Carolina sets it as a simple 1/3 of most of what the deceased spouse owned. To avoid legal tricks an Elective Share may cover items a spouse gave away recently or controlled but didn't officially own. A spouse who left and lived apart for no good reason may lose rights. An unhappy spouse might also sue for promises, like "He said I get half of things if I stayed helping while he was sick". <u>Due to all this a married person often gifts by Will and other ways mostly to a spouse (like 50% and the house)</u>. People can research their state.

YOUNG CHILD ISSUES

NAMING A PERSON LIKE A GUARDIAN TO HELP A CHILD RARELY MATTERS

A young child having parents die is rare, so parents naming people like a Guardian to help rarely matters and parents shouldn't worry too much. A study of 311,900 people found 72,240 were under 18 and of these 2014 had lost 1 parent (2.78%, or 1 in 36 children) and 97 both parents (0.13%, or 1 in 745), so losing any parent is rare and losing both 2 parents about 21 times rarer. *Parent Mortality, Census Bureau Study 288*. About half of these kids shared common parents so odds for each family are about half less than even this. It is also rare for a child to get property or money since the other parent left to raise a family usually gets all.

16

WILL CAN NAME "GUARDIAN OF THE PERSON" TO CARE FOR CHILD

If a parent dies with child under 18 other natural or adopted parents (but not step-parent) automatically then takes over control of a child's personal care, like issues with home, health care, and school unless that parent is unavailable or proven unfit in court which is rare.   But just in case it is needed a Will can name someone as "Guardian of the Person" to do this care. Since naming the other parent is pointless (they take over if fit and available) most Wills name as Guardian of the Person a friend or relative who is fairly healthy.

WILL CAN NAME "CONSERVATOR" TO MANAGE ASSETS OF CHILD

A child until 18 legally can't easily manage money or property, so in a Will a person can be named as "Conservator" to help in case a child gets things. Other states call this a "Guardian of Estate" or similar. They manage a child's money and property and pick what to pay of a child's school, health care, and living costs till usually 18 when all left goes to a child. A child's money and property must be spent only on them.

Most often because 1 parent will usually be left alive one parent usually names in Will the other parent to be Conservator, especially for rare cases a child likely may get money or property while a parent is alive. This other parent likely knows best what spending is needed and may argue with anyone else or do worse.

Less often the person named Guardian of the Person to care for a child is also named as Conservator, especially if a child will get money or property only if both parents are dead, and this can avoid some work.

Parents can also name different people, like friend or other relative maybe due to worries of drugs, theft, or bad judgment. People paying for things for a child including Guardian or Conservator can ask to be paid back from a child's money and property. Judges often hold yearly hearings looking for misuse of money.

PERSON MUST BE 18 TO HELP AND ALTERNATE PERSON RARELY IS NEEDED

A person must be at least 18 to be a Guardian or Conservator. They need not be a state resident or U.S. citizen but being local can make later work easier. Preference of last living parent has more weight. The same 1 person can be named to be Executor, Guardian, and Conservator to keep things very simple. If no Will picks person for a position or they're unavailable a judge can pick, but family may argue about this. A judge may later block a person with a bad criminal record. Naming 2 people for a position to help a child at the same time is rare since the 2 may argue and any 1 person named is trusted, but some people name a married couple. Some Wills add a second person in case first person is unavailable, but most people skip this since it is rarely needed, if seen a Will can be re-done, and a judge always can act. To add a second person words can be added like, "or if they are reasonably unable to serve I name_____ to serve".

WILLS SAY "CUSTODIAN" CAN HOLD AND SPEND MINOR'S THINGS ON THEM

Often a Will helpfully says Executor may choose to have someone be "Custodian" to get things for minor under age 18 using the "Uniform Transfers To Minor Act" law, to hold things, decide how to spend things on minor, and then give all left to them at 18 or age picked. This law was done in the 1990s to avoid problems of costs, work, and delay with Guardians and Conservators. This book's Will forms in their last paragraph says the person named in Will as Conservator or if they can't serve named as Executor may be "Custodian".

CHAPTER 6
BASIC IDEAS ABOUT HEALTH CARE FORMS

SOME BASIC IDEAS HELP USE HEALTH CARE FORMS

■ By law people control their health care unless "incapacitated" by inability to a) communicate verbally or by notes, b) be rational, or c) be conscious. Unless totally incapacitated people just tell doctor their wishes. Most people keep control of health care till death or till no big options remain, but people worry so do health care forms which mostly only matter if person is incapacitated.

■ Parents do have power over health care of child under 18. If an older person becomes incapacitated the closest family like spouse or adult child can make emergency decisions but they usually must then rush to a judge to get further power if no form names them Agent for health care.

■ In forms a person can name an "Agent" to take control later if needed or help make decisions, and naming an Agent (often spouse or adult child) can avoid family later having to rush to get power from judge.

■ In forms people can give written instructions doctors, family, and any Agent must obey, but many skip this as hard to write and it may legal issues and delay. People can give instructions but skip naming an Agent.

■ **Young people** often skip health care forms since they rarely are very ill. But some **married people** do a form to name spouse as Agent. **People 19-25** sometimes do a form just to name parents as Agents.

■ **Older people** over 40 often do form naming Agent but many skip instructions to not limit the freedom of their Agent, but people with strong wishes might write instructions carefully maybe with a doctor's help.

■ Most people do fairly long health care form with spot to name an Agent just in case this is needed, and spot for instructions. Names for the form vary. Other forms are usually only done by oldest or sickest people

■ Pain relief like pain drugs and comfort care is usually given even if forms say to stop or limit other care.

■ For rare cases stopping health care ("pulling plug") may be issue due to sick person being a) incapacitated so unable to control things, and b) in bad health with poor quality of life and little chance of recovery:

-- most people do nothing special and trust family or Agent to decide on stopping care based on changing complex factors like pain, cost, hassle, suffering and time of treatment, beliefs, and chances of recovery;

-- a few people do a serious document or just write in more plain document to block health care if **later** doctors see person has irrevocable terminal condition and see further medical care likely won't help (this action is often called doing a "Living Will" even if the form used is not titled this);

-- a few people do a serious document to **starting immediately** block health care listed, often called a "Do-Not-Resuscitate" or similar if only about "resuscitation" and restarting heart or breathing like with C.P.R., or often called a "Physician's Order" or similar if about not trying many other treatments listed in the form.

CHAPTER 7
FORM 1: LAST WILL AND TESTAMENT (STANDARD)

FORM 1 IS A STANDARD WILL THAT IS FLEXIBLE AND WITHOUT A GUARDIAN

Form 1 is a standard Will that is flexible and lets person control some things after their death. This form has no part about a Guardian or Conservator so the form is for a person with no minor child under age 18.

FORM IS WILL WITH SEVERAL PARTS

This form at start has place for person doing Will (Testator) to write their <u>full legal name</u> unless they dislike it and rarely used it, and write current county they live in (a Will is still valid if people move later).

The 1st paragraph, "Gifts", has many spaces to make either specific gifts of particular property or general gifts like of money. People can delete, copy and paste to add more, or leave blank these gift lines.

The 2nd paragraph, says to follow any separate writings done apart from the Will that gifts tangible personal property in way allowed by law.

The 3rd paragraph, "Residue", has a Residue Clause to say any property and money left after other Will parts and any other transfers is gifted to persons as the Residue Clause directs.

The 4th paragraph, "Administration", has space to name an Executor to handle legal and other matters after death, but the newer term "Personal Representative" is used here for this.

The 5th paragraph, "Miscellaneous", has paragraphs of legal language to help avoid certain legal issues.

Last is paragraph for person doing Will to sign, and paragraph for 2 witnesses to sign and put addresses.

USUAL RESIDUE CLAUSE HAS 2 PLACES TO NAME PERSONS TO GET THINGS

In a Will "Residue Clause" anything left after other Will parts is transferred as the clause directs. Many people use Residue Clause to gift most or even all things. In this Will form's Residue Clause there is:

1) a 1st space to name 1 or more persons to get the Residue, and if any named here have not survived and died before the Will maker then any other persons named here take their share,

2) a 2nd space to name people to get things if all in 1st space died before Will maker, and if any people named here didn't survive their shares go to "lineal descendants" like their children.

Most people name in 1st space a spouse or closest family or closest friends, and in 2nd space next closest family or friends. This may seem complicated but usually those in 1st area of Residue Clause get things.

TESTATOR AND 2 WITNESSES WHILE TOGETHER SIGN WILL

A Will after being filled out (except bits left blank) is signed by person doing Will (called Testator) in front of 2 witnesses who then also sign. Testator and witnesses should be in 1 room and see each person sign. Witnesses before signing quietly read just the 1 paragraph they sign. Testator can be silent and just sign but often they chat and mention the Will to help show they are acting voluntarily and are of sound mind. To be a witness a person must be at least 18 and though not required many people try to use witnesses who are local and not too old, not named in Will to get gifts, and not named in Will as Executor, Guardian, or Conservator. Having witnesses show ID and give contact information is not required but is often done.

LAST WILL AND TESTAMENT

I, _____, of _____ County, South Carolina, do revoke all prior Wills, Testaments, and Codicils, and do voluntarily make, publish, and declare this to be my Will. I am of sound mind and under no duress or undue influence.

1. GIFTS. I give these gifts in this Will, but to get a gift in this section the recipient must survive me except as otherwise stated below.

I give _____ to _____ .

I give _____ to _____ .

I give _____ to _____ .

I give _____ to _____ .

I give _____ to _____ .

I give _____ to _____ .

I give _____ to _____ .

I give _____ to _____ .

I give _____ to _____ .

I give _____ to _____ .

I give _____ to _____ .

I give _____ to _____ .

2. GIFTS OF TANGIBLE PERSONAL PROPERTY BY SEPARATE WRITINGS. I may gift tangible personal property by writings separate from a Will. Such a writing not found within 90 days of my death is canceled and of no effect. Such a writing existing when this Will is done is not revoked or canceled unless this Will specifically says this.

3. RESIDUE. I give the rest and residue and remainder of my estate, my money and property of any kind and nature, and anything I have an interest in so long as it was not transferred by other Will provisions (all of which is called the "residue"), as follows:

   a) to _____ who survive me with persons just named who survive me taking the share of non-survivors, then

   b) to _____ and if any of those just named do not survive me their part goes to their lineal descendants per stirpes.

4. ADMINISTRATION. I name and appoint _____ as Personal Representative including for me, my Will, and my estate.

5. MISCELLANEOUS. The following applies to this Will and generally.

Priority of Will gifts of the same type is based on the order they are written.

In this document no unfilled part is a mistake and residue spaces may be left blank.

The words "give" and "gift" also means a devise, bequest, grant, legacy, or similar.

A gift of property no longer owned by Testator at death shall lapse and be of no effect including no payment of money shall be done in its place, all without ademption.

If gift or gift section mentions survival, survive, or surviving then survival is an absolute condition and anti-lapse laws or similar have no effect.

Any failure to make gifts to family including children is intentional and not a mistake.

No gift or transfer made during life reduces or offsets a Will gift unless during my life I expressly usually called it a "loan" or "advancement".

Use of particular gender shall include other genders, reference to singular or plural shall be interchangeable, and "they" may be singular or plural.

Unless parts of this Will specifically says otherwise a secured debt like mortgage or lien on real property or vehicles shall not be paid off, recipient of property takes it subject to liens, and no recipient who has debtor take property or get payment via use or threat of a secured debt may require a devisee, recipient, heir, or estate to pay or do anything.

I give any Personal Representative a) the fullest authority, powers, and discretion allowed by state law, b) authority to lease, sell, mortgage, convey, or retain property including real property in any such manner and time they deem helpful or proper, and c) authority to anytime pay or settle claims or debts if they in their sole discretion chooses.

Any Personal Representative shall not be required to render and file annual or other accountings with respect to property or money including in relation to my Will or estate. Any Personal Representative may act independently in all ways without supervision.

I request informal or administrative probate of my Will and estate without supervision.

If context permits the terms Personal Representative, Executor, and Administrator shall be interchangeable as if all were written, and if context permits Conservator, Guardian of the Estate, and Guardian of Property shall be interchangeable as if all were written.

The residue includes lapsed or failed gifts, insurance paid to estate, inheritances owed me, and property I had a power of appointment or testamentary disposition over.

Any Personal Representative, Executor, Guardian of any kind, Conservator, and any fiduciary under this Will or otherwise, shall qualify and serve without bond, security,

surety, or similar, including despite place of residence or lack of ties to a state or country.

Conservator and Guardian of any kind should help all persons in my care who need it.

This Will does not revoke a Living Will or any legal document concerning health care.

A Personal Representative using their sole discretion has power at any time to transfer money or property of a child or mine or any minor to the person named Conservator in this Will to serve as Custodian under the South Carolina Uniform Transfers to Minors Act or a similar law anywhere, to serve until minor is 18, and all without bond or any court action. If they are unable to serve the person named Personal Representative shall be Custodian.

TESTATOR

IN WITNESS WHEREOF, I, _____, the Testator, publish, declare, and sign this instrument as my Will this ___ day of _____, 20____, and do hereby declare that I sign and execute this instrument as my last Will and that I sign it willingly, that I execute it as my free and voluntary act for the purposes therein expressed, and that I am 18 years of age or older, of sound mind, and under no constraint or undue influence.

_____
Testator signature

WITNESSES

We, _____ and _____, the Witnesses, sign our names to this instrument and each of us do hereby declare that the Testator willingly publishes, declares, and signs and executes this instrument as the Testator's last Will, and that each of us, in the presence and hearing of the Testator, hereby signs this Will as Witness to the Testator's signing, and that to the best of our knowledge the Testator is 18 years of age or older, of sound mind, and under no constraint or undue influence.

_____   _____
Witness signature   Witness address

_____   _____
Witness signature   Witness address

CHAPTER 8
FORM 2: LAST WILL AND TESTAMENT (GUARDIANS)

FORM 2 IS BASIC WILL WITH GUARDIANS CLAUSE FOR YOUNG CHILD

Form 2 is a Will with Guardian part and Conservator part for people with a minor child under age 18.

FORM IS WILL WITH SEVERAL PARTS

This form at start has place for person doing Will (Testator) to write their <u>full legal name</u> unless they dislike it and rarely used it, and write current county they live in (a Will is still valid if people move later).

The 1st paragraph, "Gifts", has many spaces to make either specific gifts of particular property or general gifts like of money. People can delete, copy and paste to add more, or leave blank these gift lines.

The 2nd paragraph, says to follow any separate writings done apart from the Will that gifts tangible personal property in way allowed by law.

The 3rd paragraph, "Residue", has a Residue Clause to say any property and money left after other Will parts and any other transfers is gifted to persons as the Residue Clause directs.

The 4th paragraph, "Administration", has space to name an Executor to handle legal and other matters after death, but the newer term "Personal Representative" is used here for this.

<u>The 5th paragraph, "Guardians", lets Guardian be named to care for any minor child if needed (like if no other parent is available), and lets Conservator be named to manage child's property and money if needed</u>.

The 6th paragraph, "Miscellaneous", has paragraphs of legal language to help avoid certain legal issues.

Last is paragraph for person doing Will to sign, and paragraph for 2 witnesses to sign and put addresses.

USUAL RESIDUE CLAUSE HAS 2 PLACES TO NAME PERSONS TO GET THINGS

In a Will "Residue Clause" anything left after other Will parts is transferred as the clause directs.
Many people use Residue Clause to gift most or even all things. In this Will form's Residue Clause there is:
  1) a 1st space to name 1 or more persons to get the Residue, and if any named here have not survived
     and died before the Will maker then any other persons named here take their share,
  2) a 2nd space to name people to get things if all in 1st space died before Will maker, and if any people
     named here didn't survive their shares go to "lineal descendants" like their children.
Most people name in 1st space a spouse or closest family or closest friends, and in 2nd space next closest family or friends. This may seem complicated but usually those in 1st area of Residue Clause get things.

TESTATOR AND 2 WITNESSES WHILE TOGETHER SIGN WILL

A Will after being filled out (except bits left blank) is signed by person doing Will (called Testator) in front of 2 witnesses who then also sign. Testator and witnesses should be in 1 room and see each person sign. Witnesses before signing quietly read just the 1 paragraph they sign. Testator can be silent and just sign but often they chat and mention the Will to help show they are acting voluntarily and are of sound mind. To be a witness a person must be at least 18 and though not required many people try to use witnesses who are local and not too old, not named in Will to get gifts, and not named in Will as Executor, Guardian, or Conservator. Having witnesses show ID and give contact information is not required but is often done.

LAST WILL AND TESTAMENT

I, _____, of _____ County, South Carolina, do revoke all prior Wills, Testaments, and Codicils, and do voluntarily make, publish, and declare this to be my Will. I am of sound mind and under no duress or undue influence.

1. GIFTS. I give these gifts in this Will, but to get a gift in this section the recipient must survive me except as otherwise stated below.

I give _____ to _____.

I give _____ to _____.

I give _____ to _____.

I give _____ to _____.

I give _____ to _____.

I give _____ to _____.

I give _____ to _____.

I give _____ to _____.

I give _____ to _____.

I give _____ to _____.

I give _____ to _____.

I give _____ to _____.

2. GIFTS OF TANGIBLE PERSONAL PROPERTY BY SEPARATE WRITINGS. I may gift tangible personal property by writings separate from a Will. Such a writing not found within 90 days of my death is canceled and of no effect. Such a writing existing when this Will is done is not revoked or canceled unless this Will specifically says this.

3. RESIDUE. I give the rest and residue and remainder of my estate, my money and property of any kind and nature, and anything I have an interest in so long as it was not transferred by other Will provisions (all of which is called the "residue"), as follows:

a) to _____ who survive me with persons just named who survive me taking the share of non-survivors, then

b) to _____ and if any of those just named do not survive me their part goes to their lineal descendants per stirpes.

4. ADMINISTRATION. I name and appoint _____ as Personal Representative including for me, my Will, and my estate.

5. GUARDIANS. I name and appoint _____ as Guardian to make decisions and have control of any minor child of mine's health and health care, education, maintenance, support, and personal care. I also name and appoint _____ as Conservator of any minor child of mine and their money, property, and estate.

6. MISCELLANEOUS. The following applies to this Will and generally.

Priority of Will gifts of the same type is based on the order they are written.

In this document no unfilled part is a mistake and residue spaces may be left blank.

The words "give" and "gift" also means a devise, bequest, grant, legacy, or similar.

A gift of property no longer owned by Testator at death shall lapse and be of no effect including no payment of money shall be done in its place, all without ademption.

If gift or gift section mentions survival, survive, or surviving then survival is an absolute condition and anti-lapse laws or similar have no effect.

Any failure to make gifts to family including children is intentional and not a mistake.

No gift or transfer made during life reduces or offsets a Will gift unless during my life I expressly usually called it a "loan" or "advancement".

Use of particular gender shall include other genders, reference to singular or plural shall be interchangeable, and "they" may be singular or plural.

Unless parts of this Will specifically says otherwise a secured debt like mortgage or lien on real property or vehicles shall not be paid off, recipient of property takes it subject to liens, and no recipient who has debtor take property or get payment via use or threat of a secured debt may require a devisee, recipient, heir, or estate to pay or do anything.

I give any Personal Representative a) the fullest authority, powers, and discretion allowed by state law, b) authority to lease, sell, mortgage, convey, or retain property including real property in any such manner and time they deem helpful or proper, and c) authority to anytime pay or settle claims or debts if they in their sole discretion chooses.

Any Personal Representative shall not be required to render and file annual or other accountings with respect to property or money including in relation to my Will or estate. Any Personal Representative may act independently in all ways without supervision.

I request informal or administrative probate of my Will and estate without supervision.

If context permits the terms Personal Representative, Executor, and Administrator shall be interchangeable as if all were written, and if context permits Conservator, Guardian of the Estate, and Guardian of Property shall be interchangeable as if all were written.

The residue includes lapsed or failed gifts, insurance paid to estate, inheritances owed

me, and property I had a power of appointment or testamentary disposition over.

Any Personal Representative, Executor, Guardian of any kind, Conservator, and any fiduciary under this Will or otherwise, shall qualify and serve without bond, security, surety, or similar, including despite place of residence or lack of ties to a state or country.

Conservator and Guardian of any kind should help all persons in my care who need it.

This Will does not revoke a Living Will or any legal document concerning health care.

A Personal Representative using their sole discretion has power at any time to transfer money or property of a child or mine or any minor to the person named Conservator in this Will to serve as Custodian under the South Carolina Uniform Transfers to Minors Act or a similar law anywhere, to serve until minor is 18, and all without bond or any court action. If they are unable to serve the person named Personal Representative shall be Custodian.

TESTATOR

IN WITNESS WHEREOF, I, _____, the Testator, publish, declare, and sign this instrument as my Will this ___ day of _____, 20____, and do hereby declare that I sign and execute this instrument as my last Will and that I sign it willingly, that I execute it as my free and voluntary act for the purposes therein expressed, and that I am 18 years of age or older, of sound mind, and under no constraint or undue influence.

_____
Testator signature

WITNESSES

We, _____ and _____, the Witnesses, sign our names to this instrument and each of us do hereby declare that the Testator willingly publishes, declares, and signs and executes this instrument as the Testator's last Will, and that each of us, in the presence and hearing of the Testator, hereby signs this Will as Witness to the Testator's signing, and that to the best of our knowledge the Testator is 18 years of age or older, of sound mind, and under no constraint or undue influence.

_____   _____
Witness signature   Witness address

_____   _____
Witness signature   Witness address

CHAPTER 9
FORM 3: SELF-PROVING AFFIDAVIT

FORM CAN BE DONE WITH WILL TO REDUCE LATER LEGAL WORK

This form can be done to help with later legal work involved with using a Will after a death. This form is a statutory form found in state law for people to use if wanted, and it is found at S.C. Code § 62-2-503. This book makes some minor changes to the statutory form. This form must be signed by a notary.

FORM HELPS TO LATER SHOW WILL WAS PROPERLY SIGNED

This form helps after a death when trying to use a Will to prove it was properly signed. If the form isn't done more work may be needed later, like a person who saw Will signed must do affidavit or less often testimony is gotten from people who can recognize signatures. If this form is done there is bit more risk a Will is not followed later. But a dozen states have no Self-Proving Affidavit form and manage things fine. Of people doing Wills about half skip doing a Self-Proving Affidavit mostly due to hassle of finding a notary on top of 2 witnesses each time a Will is done, and since it mostly just saves later minor work for people who are probably happy to do work to get things using a Will.

DO FORM BY TESTATOR AND 1 OR 2 WITNESSES SIGNING WITH A NOTARY

To complete the form the person who did Will as Testator and at least 1 person who witnessed Will must sign the form in front of a notary who then notarizes it. South Carolina only requires 1 person who witnessed a Will signing do the form but many people to be safer have both 2 witnesses sign the form. The form is often done within minutes of when Will is signed but it also can be done anytime later (even many months later) when Testator and 1 or 2 witnesses can meet a notary to do the Self-Proving Affidavit. A notary can be found and asked to help at banks, insurance agents, some government offices, libraries, and courts, but they often are busy and choose to not help. Often people find a helpful notary by using a phonebook and paying for help. Once done the Self-Proving Affidavit if often kept with the Will it supports.

SELF-PROVING AFFIDAVIT

(S.C. Code § 62-2-503)

State of South Carolina

County of _____

We, _____ and _____,
the Testator and at least one of the Witnesses (a second Witness also can be named here
and do this form), respectively, whose names are signed to the attached or foregoing
instrument, being first duly sworn, do hereby declare to the undersigned authority that

    the Testator signed and executed the instrument as their last Will and that they had
signed willingly, and that they executed it as their free and voluntary act for the purposes
therein expressed, and

    that each of the Witnesses, in the presence and hearing of the Testator, signed the Will
as Witness and to the best of their knowledge the testator was at that time 18 years of age
or older, of sound mind, and under no constraint or undue influence.

_____

Testator

_____

Witness(es)

Subscribed, sworn to, and acknowledged before me by _____,
the Testator, and subscribed and sworn to before me by one or more Witnesses,

_____, this ___ day of _____, 20___.

_____

NOTARY PUBLIC FOR SOUTH CAROLINA
My Commission Expires:_____

CHAPTER 10
FORM 4: TANGIBLE PERSONAL PROPERTY LIST

LETS GIFTS OF SOME PROPERTY BE EASILY MADE OUTSIDE A WILL

This form lets people before or after Will is done easily add some gifts of property they want to occur after their death. This form is often called a "Memorandum", "Gift List", or often just "List"

FORM GIVES EASY QUICK WAY TO WRITE GIFTS

The form in this Chapter, often just called the List form, lets person before or after Will has been done easily write more gifts of property to occur after their death without hassle of doing a new Will. For a List to be used a Will must say they can be used, and this book's Will forms say this. This book's Will forms also say any existing List is not revoked by the Will. If List and Will gift the same item by law the Will is followed. People can do many List pages over time and all can count. If multiple Lists gift the same item the more recently done List controls. People can change Lists by crossing out, erasing, or adding words, but people then should put new date and signature at bottom. To cut uncertainty this book's forms say a List not found within 90 days of death is ignored. People to cancel List can rip it, mark it like "void" or "X", or throw it away.

It may help understanding to show the South Carolina law allowing Lists, which says:

"**SECTION 62-2-512. Separate writing identifying bequest of tangible property.**

A will may refer to a written statement or list to dispose of items of tangible personal property not otherwise specifically disposed of by the will, other than money and property used in trade or business.

To be admissible under this section as evidence of the intended disposition, the writing must either be in the handwriting of the testator or be signed by the testator and must describe the items and the devisees with reasonable certainty.

The writing may be referred to as one to be in existence at the time of the testator's death; it may be prepared before or after the execution of the will; it may be altered by the testator after its preparation; and it may be a writing that has no significance apart from its effect upon the dispositions made by the will."

FORM CAN ONLY GIFT "TANGIBLE PERSONAL PROPERTY"

The List form can gift only "tangible personal property", so only tangible (touchable) things so not most accounts or investments, and not "real property" (land or buildings). It can't cover cash or coins even if old. It can't cover items used in a business including inventory. Improper property written in a form is ignored.

TO COMPLETE GIFT LIST A PERSON JUST SIGNS AND DATES IT

To be valid a List form just must be signed and dated by the person who is doing the form. Once they are completed List form pages are often kept with a Will.

TANGIBLE PERSONAL PROPERTY LIST

In this writing are gifts of tangible personal property to occur at my death, but this writing if not found by someone within 90 days of my death is void and canceled.

I may do many of these writings which should be seen as a single document with the more recent writing controlling if any gifts conflict.

If a person getting a gift below does not survive me such gift is void and canceled.

PROPERTY ITEMS   **NAMES OF RECIPIENTS**

_____ to _____

_____ to _____

_____ to _____

_____ to _____

_____ to _____

_____ to _____

_____ to _____

_____ to _____

_____ to _____

_____ to _____

_____ to _____

_____ to _____

_____ to _____

_____ to _____

_____ to _____

_____ to _____

_____ to _____

DATE:_____   SIGNED:_____

CHAPTER 11
FORM 5: HEALTH CARE POWER OF ATTORNEY

FORM CAN COVER SOME HEALTH CARE ISSUES

This form lets person do some things involving health care issues. This form is a statutory form found in state law for people to use if wanted, and it is found at S.C. Code § 62-5-504. This form is often the only Estate Planning form about health care that people in South Carolina do.

CAN NAME "HEALTH CARE AGENT" AND GIVE INSTRUCTIONS

Form lets "Health Care Agent" be named to have power to control health care in case person doing form is ever incapacitated so can't control health care themselves. Often named Agent is spouse, adult child, relative, or friend. Naming a family member can avoid need to rush to see judge for power in an emergency. A person who is Agent can see health care records and talk to doctors and give orders. People associated with a place giving care can't normally be Agent for a person unless they are a relative or spouse of relative. There is a spot to name additional people to serve if first person is unavailable but many people don't bother since it is rarely needed. The form also has room to give health care instructions, but many people skip this since it's hard to write for all situations clearly enough to not risk legal problems or delays, and they trust Agent or family to be wise or do as discussed. Family and Agent should do what a sick person would want.

IN FORM A PERSON CAN SAY WHEN TO STOP CARE OR CAN SKIP THIS

The form's last half covers stopping health care if later a person is incapacitated and doctors or family think their health is very bad and unlikely to improve. Doing this is often called a "Living Will". If people want they can cover stopping care in this Health Care Power Of Attorney form by initialing options in area 7 and area 8. But usually people handle stopping care in a separate form (see next Chapter's form) which if done overrides anything else written on this issue. But most people skip saying when to stop care in any way since it is a difficult issue, it rarely matters, and people just trust Agent or family to act wisely.

PERSON SIGNS FORM IN FRONT OF 2 WITNESSES

To complete the form a person signs in front of 2 persons acting as witnesses who then also sign form. People to be witnesses must be at least 18, not named as Health Care Agent in form, not related to person doing the form by blood, marriage, or adoption, and not somehow responsible for paying for health care. Persons acting as witnesses must not think they'll benefit from death of person doing the form either by being named in a Will gift, named in insurance, or likely to collect on a debt. A person acting as a witness can't be the attending physician or their employee, and only 1 person who is a witness can be in any way working for a health care facility giving some care. Once it is done a person can keep the form but most people immediately hand it to the Agent or family members to have. Usually this form should quickly be shown to any doctor or place that may give care to make it part of a person's medical file to then follow. To cancel the form a person should tell any Health Care Agent named in the form and take back copies and then usually tell any place shown the form it is canceled.

SOUTH CAROLINA
HEALTH CARE POWER OF ATTORNEY

INFORMATION ABOUT THIS DOCUMENT

THIS IS AN IMPORTANT LEGAL DOCUMENT. BEFORE SIGNING THIS DOCUMENT, YOU SHOULD KNOW THESE IMPORTANT FACTS:

1. THIS DOCUMENT GIVES THE PERSON YOU NAME AS YOUR AGENT THE POWER TO MAKE HEALTH CARE DECISIONS FOR YOU IF YOU CANNOT MAKE THE DECISION FOR YOURSELF. THIS POWER INCLUDES THE POWER TO MAKE DECISIONS ABOUT LIFE-SUSTAINING TREATMENT. UNLESS YOU STATE OTHERWISE, YOUR AGENT WILL HAVE THE SAME AUTHORITY TO MAKE DECISIONS ABOUT YOUR HEALTH CARE AS YOU WOULD HAVE.

2. THIS POWER IS SUBJECT TO ANY LIMITATIONS OR STATEMENTS OF YOUR DESIRES THAT YOU INCLUDE IN THIS DOCUMENT. YOU MAY STATE IN THIS DOCUMENT ANY TREATMENT YOU DO NOT DESIRE OR TREATMENT YOU WANT TO BE SURE YOU RECEIVE. YOUR AGENT WILL BE OBLIGATED TO FOLLOW YOUR INSTRUCTIONS WHEN MAKING DECISIONS ON YOUR BEHALF. YOU MAY ATTACH ADDITIONAL PAGES IF YOU NEED MORE SPACE TO COMPLETE THE STATEMENT.

3. AFTER YOU HAVE SIGNED THIS DOCUMENT, YOU HAVE THE RIGHT TO MAKE HEALTH CARE DECISIONS FOR YOURSELF IF YOU ARE MENTALLY COMPETENT TO DO SO. AFTER YOU HAVE SIGNED THIS DOCUMENT, NO TREATMENT MAY BE GIVEN TO YOU OR STOPPED OVER YOUR OBJECTION IF YOU ARE MENTALLY COMPETENT TO MAKE THAT DECISION.

4. YOU HAVE THE RIGHT TO REVOKE THIS DOCUMENT, AND TERMINATE YOUR AGENT'S AUTHORITY, BY INFORMING EITHER YOUR AGENT OR YOUR HEALTH CARE PROVIDER ORALLY OR IN WRITING.

5. IF THERE IS ANYTHING IN THIS DOCUMENT THAT YOU DO NOT UNDERSTAND, YOU SHOULD ASK A SOCIAL WORKER, LAWYER, OR OTHER PERSON TO EXPLAIN IT TO YOU.

6. THIS POWER OF ATTORNEY WILL NOT BE VALID UNLESS TWO PERSONS SIGN AS WITNESSES. EACH OF THESE PERSONS MUST EITHER WITNESS YOUR SIGNING OF THE POWER OF ATTORNEY OR WITNESS YOUR ACKNOWLEDGMENT THAT THE SIGNATURE ON THE POWER OF ATTORNEY IS YOURS.

THE FOLLOWING PERSONS MAY NOT ACT AS WITNESSES:

A. YOUR SPOUSE, YOUR CHILDREN, GRANDCHILDREN, AND OTHER LINEAL DESCENDANTS; YOUR PARENTS, GRANDPARENTS, AND OTHER LINEAL

ANCESTORS; YOUR SIBLINGS AND THEIR LINEAL DESCENDANTS; OR A SPOUSE OF ANY OF THESE PERSONS.

B. A PERSON WHO IS DIRECTLY FINANCIALLY RESPONSIBLE FOR YOUR MEDICAL CARE.

C. A PERSON WHO IS NAMED IN YOUR WILL, OR, IF YOU HAVE NO WILL, WHO WOULD INHERIT YOUR PROPERTY BY INTESTATE SUCCESSION.

D. BENEFICIARY OF A LIFE INSURANCE POLICY ON YOUR LIFE.

E. THE PERSONS NAMED IN THE HEALTH CARE POWER OF ATTORNEY AS YOUR AGENT OR SUCCESSOR AGENT.

F. YOUR PHYSICIAN OR AN EMPLOYEE OF YOUR PHYSICIAN.

G. A PERSON WHO WOULD HAVE A CLAIM AGAINST ANY PORTION OF YOUR ESTATE (PERSONS TO WHOM YOU OWE MONEY).

IF YOU ARE A PATIENT IN A HEALTH FACILITY, NO MORE THAN ONE WITNESS MAY BE AN EMPLOYEE OF THAT FACILITY.

7. YOUR AGENT MUST BE A PERSON WHO IS 18 YEARS OF AGE OR OLDER AND OF SOUND MIND. IT MAY NOT BE YOUR DOCTOR OR ANY OTHER HEALTH CARE PROVIDER THAT IS NOW PROVIDING YOU WITH TREATMENT; OR AN EMPLOYEE OF YOUR DOCTOR OR PROVIDER; OR A SPOUSE OF THE DOCTOR, PROVIDER, OR EMPLOYEE; UNLESS THE PERSON IS A RELATIVE OF YOURS.

8. YOU SHOULD INFORM THE PERSON THAT YOU WANT HIM OR HER TO BE YOUR HEALTH CARE AGENT. YOU SHOULD DISCUSS THIS DOCUMENT WITH YOUR AGENT AND YOUR PHYSICIAN AND GIVE EACH A SIGNED COPY. IF YOU ARE IN A HEALTH CARE FACILITY OR A NURSING CARE FACILITY, A COPY OF THIS DOCUMENT SHOULD BE INCLUDED IN YOUR MEDICAL RECORD.

HEALTH CARE POWER OF ATTORNEY

1. DESIGNATION OF HEALTH CARE AGENT

I, _____ (Principal), hereby appoint:
_____ (Agent's Name)
_____ (Agent's Address)
Telephone: home: _____ work: _____ mobile: _____
as my agent to make health care decisions for me as authorized in this document.

Successor Agent: If an agent named by me dies, becomes legally disabled, resigns, refuses to act, becomes unavailable, or if an agent who is my spouse is divorced or separated from me, I name the following as successors to my agent, each to act alone and successively, in the order named:

A. First Alternate Agent:
Address: _____
Telephone: home: _____ work: _____ mobile: _____

B. Second Alternate Agent:
Address: _____
Telephone: home: _____ work: _____ mobile: _____

Unavailability of Agent(s): If at any relevant time the agent or successor agents named here are unable or unwilling to make decisions concerning my health care, and those decisions are to be made by a guardian, by the Probate Court, or by a surrogate pursuant to the Adult Health Care Consent Act, it is my intention that the guardian, Probate Court, or surrogate make those decisions in accordance with my directions as stated in this document.

2. EFFECTIVE DATE AND DURABILITY

By this document I intend to create a durable power of attorney effective upon, and only during, any period of mental incompetence, except as provided in Paragraph 3 below.

3. HIPAA AUTHORIZATION

When considering or making health care decisions for me, all individually identifiable health information and medical records may be released without restriction to my health care agent(s) and/or my alternate health care agent(s) named above including, but not limited to, (i) diagnostic, treatment, other health care, and related insurance and financial records and information associated with any past, present, or future physical or mental health condition including, but not limited to, diagnosis or treatment of HIV/AIDS, sexually transmitted disease(s), mental illness, and/or drug or alcohol abuse and (ii) any written opinion relating to my health that such health care agent(s) and/or alternate health care agent(s) may have requested. Without limiting the generality of the foregoing, this release authority applies to all health information and medical records governed by the Health Insurance Portability and Accountability Act of 1996 (HIPAA), 42 U.S.C. 1320d and 45 C.F.R. 160-164; is effective whether or not I am mentally competent; has no expiration date; and shall terminate only in the event that I revoke the authority in writing and deliver it to my health care provider.

4. AGENT'S POWERS

I grant to my agent full authority to make decisions for me regarding my health care. In exercising this authority, my agent shall follow my desires as stated in this document or otherwise expressed by me or known to my agent. In making any decision, my agent shall attempt to discuss the proposed decision with me to determine my desires if I am able to communicate in any way. If my agent cannot determine the choice I would want made, then my agent shall make a choice for me based upon what my agent believes to be in my best interests. My agent's authority to interpret my desires is intended to be as broad as possible, except for any limitations I may state below.

Accordingly, unless specifically limited by the provisions specified below, my agent is authorized as follows:

A. To consent, refuse, or withdraw consent to any and all types of medical care, treatment, surgical procedures, diagnostic procedures, medication, and the use of mechanical or other procedures that affect any bodily function, including, but not limited to, artificial respiration, nutritional support and hydration, and cardiopulmonary resuscitation.

B. To authorize, or refuse to authorize, any medication or procedure intended to relieve pain, even though that use may lead to physical damage, addiction, or hasten the moment of, but not intentionally cause, my death.

C. To authorize my admission to or discharge, even against medical advice, from a hospital, nursing care facility, or similar facility or service.

D. To take another action necessary to making, documenting, and assuring implementation of decisions concerning my health care, including, but not limited to, granting a waiver or release from liability required by a hospital, physician, nursing care provider, or other health care provider; signing any documents relating to refusals of treatment or the leaving of a facility against medical advice, and pursuing any legal action in my name, and at the expense of my estate to force compliance with my wishes as determined by my agent, or to seek actual or punitive damages for the failure to comply.

E. The powers granted above do not include the following powers or are subject to the following rules or limitations:_____

_____

_____

_____

_____

_____

_____

_____

_____

5. ORGAN DONATION (INITIAL ONLY ONE)
My agent may _____; may not _____ consent to the donation of all or any of my tissue or organs for purposes of transplantation.

6. EFFECT ON DECLARATION OF A DESIRE FOR A NATURAL DEATH (LIVING WILL)
I understand that if I have a valid Declaration of a Desire for a Natural Death, the instructions contained in the Declaration will be given effect in any situation to which they are applicable. My agent will have authority to make decisions concerning my health care only in situations to which the Declaration does not apply.

7. STATEMENT OF DESIRES CONCERNING LIFE-SUSTAINING TREATMENT
With respect to any Life-Sustaining Treatment, I direct the following:
(INITIAL ONLY ONE OF THE FOLLOWING 3 PARAGRAPHS)
A. _____ **GRANT OF DISCRETION TO AGENT.** I do not want my life to be prolonged nor do I want life-sustaining treatment to be provided or continued if my agent believes the burdens of the treatment outweigh the expected benefits. I want my agent to consider the relief of suffering, my personal beliefs, the expense involved and the quality as well as the possible extension of my life in making decisions concerning life-sustaining treatment.

OR

B. _____ DIRECTIVE TO WITHHOLD OR WITHDRAW TREATMENT. I do not want
my life to be prolonged and I do not want life-sustaining treatment:
1. if I have a condition that is incurable or irreversible and, without the administration of life-sustaining procedures, expected to result in death within a relatively short period of time; or
2. if I am in a state of permanent unconsciousness.

OR

C. _____ DIRECTIVE FOR MAXIMUM TREATMENT. I want my life to be prolonged
to the greatest extent possible, within the standards of accepted medical practice, without regard
to my condition, the chances I have for recovery, or the cost of the procedures.

8. STATEMENT OF DESIRES REGARDING TUBE FEEDING

With respect to Nutrition and Hydration provided by means of a nasogastric tube or tube into
the stomach, intestines, or veins, I wish to make clear that in situations where life-sustaining
treatment is being withheld or withdrawn pursuant to Paragraph 7:

(INITIAL ONLY ONE OF THE FOLLOWING 3 PARAGRAPHS):

A. _____ GRANT OF DISCRETION TO AGENT. I do not want my life to be prolonged by
tube feeding if my agent believes the burdens of tube feeding outweigh the expected benefits. I
want my agent to consider the relief of suffering, my personal beliefs, the expense involved, and
the quality as well as the possible extension of my life in making this decision.

OR

B. _____ DIRECTIVE TO WITHHOLD OR WITHDRAW TUBE FEEDING. I do not
want my life prolonged by tube feeding.

OR

C. _____ DIRECTIVE FOR PROVISION OF TUBE FEEDING. I want tube feeding to be
provided within the standards of accepted medical practice, without regard to my condition, the
chances I have for recovery, or the cost of the procedure, and without regard to whether other
forms of life-sustaining treatment are being withheld or withdrawn.

**IF YOU DO NOT INITIAL ANY OF THE STATEMENTS IN PARAGRAPH 8, YOUR
AGENT WILL NOT HAVE AUTHORITY TO DIRECT THAT NUTRITION AND
HYDRATION NECESSARY FOR COMFORT CARE OR ALLEVIATION OF PAIN BE
WITHDRAWN.**

9. ADMINISTRATIVE PROVISIONS

A. I revoke any prior Health Care Power of Attorney and any provisions relating to health care
of any other prior power of attorney.
B. This power of attorney is intended to be valid in any jurisdiction in which it is presented.

BY SIGNING HERE I INDICATE THAT I UNDERSTAND THE CONTENTS OF THIS DOCUMENT AND THE EFFECT OF THIS GRANT OF POWERS TO MY AGENT.

I sign my name to this Health Care Power of Attorney on this __ day of _____, 20 __.
My current home address is:_____

    Principal's Signature: _____

    Print Name of Principal: _____

I declare, on the basis of information and belief, that the person who signed or acknowledged this document (the principal) is personally known to me, that he/she signed or acknowledged this Health Care Power of Attorney in my presence, and that he/she appears to be of sound mind and under no duress, fraud, or undue influence. I am not related to the principal by blood, marriage, or adoption, either as a spouse, a lineal ancestor, descendant of the parents of the principal, or spouse of any of them. I am not directly financially responsible for the principal's medical care. I am not entitled to any portion of the principal's estate upon his decease, whether under any will or as an heir by intestate succession, nor am I the beneficiary of an insurance policy on the principal's life, nor do I have a claim against the principal's estate as of this time. I am not the principal's attending physician, nor an employee of the attending physician. No more than one witness is an employee of a health care facility in which the principal is a patient. I am not appointed as Health Care Agent or Successor Health Care Agent by this document.

Witness No. 1
Signature: _____ Date: _____

Print Name: _____ Telephone: _____

Address: _____

Witness No. 2
Signature: _____ Date: _____

Print Name: _____ Telephone: _____

Address: _____

    (This portion of the document is optional and is not required to create a valid health care power of attorney.)

STATE OF SOUTH CAROLINA

COUNTY OF _____

The foregoing instrument was acknowledged before me by Principal on _____, 20__.

Notary Public for South Carolina _____
My Commission Expires: _____

CHAPTER 12
FORM 6: DECLARATION OF A DESIRE FOR A NATURAL DEATH

IN FORM CAN REFUSE FURTHER MEDICAL CARE IF LATER BADLY ILL

This form lets person give instructions about stopping health care if they are later badly ill. This long form is hard to read fast and is more often used <u>inside</u> hospitals or similar places. This form is mostly done only by sickest or oldest people and most people skip this form. This form only matters if a person is later incapacitated. This form is a statutory form found in state law, and it is located at S.C. Code § 44-77-50.

FORM SAYS STOP CARE IF LATER DOCTORS THINK HEALTH WILL STAY BAD

This form lets person say to stop health care if <u>later</u> the <u>doctors think an incapacitated person has very bad health</u> and <u>more care likely won't help</u>. This form only matters if a person is incapacitated so can't control things themselves due to inability to stay conscious, be rational enough, or communicate enough. The form has options about how bad must later health be and what kinds of care to stop. Hospitals and similar places may have a similar form they prefer. The person doing this form is called the "Declarant". This form overrides any instructions about stopping care found in a Health Care Power Of Attorney form.

PERSON AND 2 WITNESSES MUST SIGN FORM IN FRONT OF A NOTARY

To complete the form a person signs in front of 2 witnesses who then sign and a notary who notarizes the form. People to be witnesses must be at least 18 and can't be spouse, parent, or child of person doing form, and also not financially responsible for the person's care, and also not likely to benefit and get things in the person's Will or similar gift. The notary can sign as 1 of the 2 witnesses but this option is rarely used. The completed form usually is shown to places that may give care to make it part of a person's medical file. To cancel the form a person usually should tell all places shown the form that it is canceled.

DECLARATION OF A DESIRE FOR A NATURAL DEATH

STATE OF SOUTH CAROLINA   COUNTY OF _____

I, _____ , Social Security Number _____, being at least 18 years of age and a resident of and domiciled in the City of _____, County of _____, State of South Carolina, make this Declaration this __ day of _____, 20__.

I wilfully and voluntarily make known my desire that no life-sustaining procedures be used to prolong my dying if my condition is terminal or if I am in a state of permanent unconsciousness, and I declare:

If at any time I have a condition certified to be a terminal condition by two physicians who have personally examined me, one of whom is my attending physician, and the physicians have determined that my death could occur within a reasonably short period of time without the use of life-sustaining procedures or if the physicians certify that I am in a state of permanent unconsciousness and where the application of life-sustaining procedures would serve only to prolong the dying process, I direct that the procedures be withheld or withdrawn, and that I be permitted to die naturally with only the administration of medication or the performance of any medical procedure necessary to provide me with comfort care.

INSTRUCTIONS CONCERNING ARTIFICIAL NUTRITION AND HYDRATION
INITIAL ONE OF THE FOLLOWING STATEMENTS
If my condition is <u>terminal</u> and could result in death within a reasonably short time,
_____ I direct that nutrition and hydration BE PROVIDED through any medically indicated means, including medically or surgically implanted tubes.
_____ I direct that nutrition and hydration NOT BE PROVIDED through any medically indicated means, including medically or surgically implanted tubes.

INITIAL ONE OF THE FOLLOWING STATEMENTS
If I am in a <u>persistent vegetative state</u> or other condition of permanent unconsciousness,
_____ I direct that nutrition and hydration BE PROVIDED through any medically indicated means, including medically or surgically implanted tubes.
_____ I direct that nutrition and hydration NOT BE PROVIDED through any medically indicated means, including medically or surgically implanted tubes.

In the absence of my ability to give directions regarding the use of life-sustaining procedures, it is my intention that this Declaration be honored by my family and physicians and any health facility in which I may be a patient as the final expression of my legal right to refuse medical or surgical treatment, and I accept the consequences from the refusal.

I am aware that this Declaration authorizes a physician to withhold or withdraw life-sustaining procedures. I am emotionally and mentally competent to make this Declaration.

APPOINTMENT OF AN AGENT (OPTIONAL)

1. You may give another person authority to <u>revoke</u> this declaration on your behalf. If you wish to do so, please enter that person's name in the space below.

Name of Agent with Power to Revoke:_____ Phone:_____
Address:_____

2. You may give another person authority to <u>enforce</u> this declaration on your behalf. If you wish to do so, please enter that person's name in the space below.

Name of Agent with Power to Revoke:_____ Phone:_____
Address:_____

REVOCATION PROCEDURES

THIS DECLARATION MAY BE REVOKED BY ANY ONE OF THE FOLLOWING METHODS. HOWEVER, A REVOCATION IS NOT EFFECTIVE UNTIL IT IS COMMUNICATED TO THE ATTENDING PHYSICIAN.

(1) BY BEING DEFACED, TORN, OBLITERATED, OR OTHERWISE DESTROYED, IN EXPRESSION OF YOUR INTENT TO REVOKE, BY YOU OR BY SOME PERSON IN YOUR PRESENCE AND BY YOUR DIRECTION. REVOCATION BY DESTRUCTION OF ONE OR MORE OF MULTIPLE ORIGINAL DECLARATIONS REVOKES ALL OF THE ORIGINAL DECLARATIONS;

(2) BY A WRITTEN REVOCATION SIGNED AND DATED BY YOU EXPRESSING YOUR INTENT TO REVOKE;

(3) BY YOUR ORAL EXPRESSION OF YOUR INTENT TO REVOKE THE DECLARATION. AN ORAL REVOCATION COMMUNICATED TO THE ATTENDING PHYSICIAN BY A PERSON OTHER THAN YOU IS EFFECTIVE ONLY IF:
   (a) THE PERSON WAS PRESENT WHEN THE ORAL REVOCATION WAS MADE;
   (b) THE REVOCATION WAS COMMUNICATED TO THE PHYSICIAN WITHIN A REASONABLE TIME;
   (c) YOUR PHYSICAL OR MENTAL CONDITION MAKES IT IMPOSSIBLE FOR THE PHYSICIAN TO CONFIRM THROUGH SUBSEQUENT CONVERSATION WITH YOU THAT THE REVOCATION HAS OCCURRED.

TO BE EFFECTIVE AS A REVOCATION, THE ORAL EXPRESSION CLEARLY MUST INDICATE YOUR DESIRE THAT THE DECLARATION NOT BE GIVEN EFFECT OR THAT LIFE-SUSTAINING PROCEDURES BE ADMINISTERED;

(4) IF YOU, IN THE SPACE ABOVE, HAVE AUTHORIZED AN AGENT TO REVOKE THE DECLARATION, THE AGENT MAY REVOKE ORALLY OR BY A WRITTEN, SIGNED, AND DATED INSTRUMENT. AN AGENT MAY REVOKE ONLY IF YOU ARE INCOMPETENT TO DO SO. AN AGENT MAY REVOKE THE DECLARATION PERMANENTLY OR TEMPORARILY.

(5) BY YOUR EXECUTING ANOTHER DECLARATION AT A LATER TIME.

Signature of Declarant:_____

AFFIDAVIT

STATE OF SOUTH CAROLINA, COUNTY OF _____

We, _____ and _____, the undersigned witnesses
to the foregoing Declaration, dated the __ day of _____, 20__, at least one of us being
first duly sworn, declare to the undersigned authority, on the basis of our best information and
belief, that the Declaration was on that date signed by the declarant as and for his
DECLARATION OF A DESIRE FOR A NATURAL DEATH in our presence and we, at his
request and in his presence, and in the presence of each other, subscribe our names as witnesses
on that date. The declarant is personally known to us, and we believe him to be of sound mind.
Each of us affirms that he is qualified as a witness to this Declaration under the provisions of the
South Carolina Death With Dignity Act in that he is not related to the declarant by blood,
marriage, or adoption, either as a spouse, lineal ancestor, descendant of the parents of the
declarant, or spouse of any of them; nor directly financially responsible for the declarant's
medical care; nor entitled to any portion of the declarant's estate upon his decease, whether
under any will or as an heir by intestate succession; nor the beneficiary of a life insurance policy
of the declarant; nor the declarant's attending physician; nor an employee of the attending
physician; nor a person who has a claim against the declarant's decedent's estate as of this time.
No more than one of us is an employee of a health facility in which the declarant is a patient.
If the declarant is a resident in a hospital or nursing care facility at the date of execution of this
Declaration, at least one of us is an ombudsman designated by the State Ombudsman, Office of
the Governor.

_____ Witness

_____ Witness

Subscribed before me by _____, the declarant, and subscribed and sworn
to before me by _____ and _____, the witnesses, this
__ day of _____, 20__.

Signature of Notary Public:_____

Notary Public for South Carolina
My commission expires: _____   SEAL

CHAPTER 13
FORM 7: DO NOT RESUSCITATE ORDER

IN THESE FORMS A PERSON CAN REFUSE CARE STARTING IMMEDIATELY

This Chapter covers 2 similar forms. Forms in this chapter say to immediately no longer try certain medical treatments listed in the forms. These forms are rarely done and usually only by very sick or very old people in bad medical condition. A person usually does not do both these 2 forms. These forms only matter if a person is later incapacitated. These forms are short and can be read fast and used outside a hospital or similar places, but these forms can also be used inside these places too.

D.N.R. FORM SAYS TO NOT "RESUSCITATE" STARTING IMMEDIATELY

The Do Not Resuscitate Order form is often called a "D.N.R." form. This form says immediately to not try to "resuscitate" which means try to restart or aid breathing or heart by hand or mouth (C.P.R.), electrically (shock or defibrillator), or mechanically (tube, mask, or machine). C.P.R. is cardio-pulmonary resuscitation. Pain relief and comfort care is usually still given, so a person falling sick is still usually taken to get this care. After doing form a person if still rational can override it by saying so or not showing form like to paramedics. By law to use a D.N.R. form a person must be in "terminal condition" which means they have an incurable or irreversible condition doctors think will cause death in a short time if life sustaining procedures are not used. People in a hospital or similar places can do a "Do Not Intubate" form to clearly block use of a throat air tube.

P.O.S.T. FORMS SAYS TO NOT DO OTHER CARE STARTING IMMEDIATELY

This Chapter also shows the "Physician Orders For Scope Of Treatment" form, often called "P.O.S.T." form, which says to immediately do not try any of the many kinds care listed in form (not just resuscitation). This form is short enough to be used outside a hospital or similar places but is often used inside places too. The P.O.S.T. form is now used more often than the D.N.R. form and is often confused with the other form.

FORMS IN THIS CHAPTER MUST SIGNED BY PERSON AND THEIR DOCTOR

The D.N.R. and the P.O.S.T. form must be signed by a person and also their doctor or similar health professional. If a person is already incapacitated a person's family or Health Care Agent can do these forms if it's what a person would want. A completed form should be shown to places that may give care to put in person's medical file. A person often keeps the form near to show paramedics or similar people who may try to give health care (for example in wallet, pinned to shirt, on bedside table, or on home refrigerator). Some people buy a metal bracelet to wear from special companies (like from StickyJ Medical Company located in Florida but people should ensure it's the "South Carolina D.N.R. Bracelet"). To cancel one of these forms people can tell a doctor or nurse and then usually tell all places shown the form it is canceled.

Emergency Medical Services
Do Not Resuscitate Order

SOUTH CAROLINA
EMERGENCY MEDICAL SERVICES

RESUSCITATE

DO NOT RESUSCITATE ORDER

NOTICE TO EMS PERSONNEL

This notice is to inform all emergency medical personnel who may be called to render assistance to

_____ that he/she has a terminal condition which has been diagnosed by me
(Name of Patient)

and has specifically requested, or a parent or legal guardian with the authority to make medical decisions for a child has

requested that no resuscitative efforts including artificial stimulation of the cardiopulmonary system by electrical,

mechanical, or manual means be made in the event of cardiopulmonary arrest.

REVOCATION PROCEDURE

**THIS FORM MAY BE REVOKED BY AN ORAL STATEMENT BY THE PATIENT TO EMS PERSONNEL, OR BY
MUTILATING, OBLITERATING, OR DESTROYING THE DOCUMENT IN ANY MANNER.**

_____   _____
Date   Patient's Signature (or Surrogate or Agent)

_____   _____
Physician's/ APRN's/ PA's Name (Please Print)   Physician's/ APRN's/ PA's Signature

_____   _____
Physician's/ APRN's/ PA's Address   Physician's/ APRN's/ PA's Telephone Number

DHEC 3462 (01/2020)   **SOUTH CAROLINA DEPARTMENT OF HEALTH AND ENVIRONMENTAL CONTROL**

DNR INFORMATION FOR THE PATIENT, THE PATIENT'S FAMILY, PHYSICIAN, ADVANCED PRACTICE REGISTERED NURSE (APRN), PHYSICIAN ASSISTANT (PA), AND EMS PERSONNEL

1. Responsibilities of the Patient or his/her Surrogate or Agent
    The patient and his/her surrogate or agent:

    Will make all care givers aware of the location of the EMS DNR Form and will ensure that the form is displayed in such a manner that it will be visible and available to EMS personnel;

    Understanding the consequences of refusing resuscitative measures;

    Are aware that if the form is altered in any manner resuscitative measures will be initiated; and

    Understand that in all cases, supportive care will be provided to the patient.

2. Responsibilities of the Health Physician
    The patient's physician, APRN, or PA:

    Has determined that the patient has a terminal condition;

    Has completed the patient's EMS DNR Form;

    Has explained to the patient and family the consequences of withholding resuscitative care; the medical procedures that will be withheld and the palliative and supportive care that will be administrated to the patient; and

    Must execute the DNR order pursuant to the provisions of the Emergency Medical Services Do Not Resuscitate Order Act in accordance with their respective practice acts.

3. Responsibilities of EMS Personnel
    EMS personnel:

    Will confirm the presence of the EMS DNR Form and the identity of the Patient;

    Upon finding an unaltered EMS DNR Form, will withhold or withdraw resuscitative measures such as CPR, endotracheal intubation or other advanced airway management, artificial ventilation, defibrillation, cardiac resuscitation medication and related procedures;

    Will provide palliative and supportive treatment such as suctioning the airway, administration of oxygen, control bleeding, provision of pain and non-cardiac medications, provide comfort care and provide emotional support for the patient and the patient's family; and

    Will assure that the DNR Form accompanies the patient during transport.

THIS PAGE INTENTIONALLY BLANK

dhec	**Patient Last Name:**
	Patient First Name/MI:
South Carolina **Physician Orders for Scope of Treatment (POST)**	**Patient Date of Birth:** (MM/DD/YYYY)
	Patient/Legal Representative Phone Number:
	Social Security Number last 4 digits: *(Optional)* XXX-XX-
	Gender: ☐ M ☐ F ☐ Other
	Patient Mailing Address: (street/city/state/zip)
Patient's Diagnosis:	

Section A *Check One Box Only*	**CARDIOPULMONARY RESUSCITATION (CPR): Unresponsive, pulseless, & not breathing.**
	☐ **Attempt Resuscitation/CPR** (Selecting CPR requires Full Treatment in Section B.) ☐ **Do Not Attempt Resuscitation/DNR** (Allow <u>N</u>atural <u>D</u>eath.) *If patient is not in cardiopulmonary arrest, follow orders in B, C and D.*

Section B *Check One Box Only*	**MEDICAL INTERVENTIONS: If patient has pulse and/or is breathing.**
	☐ **Full Treatment.** In addition to care described in Comfort Measures Only and Limited Treatment, use intubation, advanced airway interventions, mechanical ventilation, and cardioversion as indicated. ***Transfer to hospital and/or intensive care unit if indicated.*** <u>**Treatment Plan: All treatments including breathing machine.**</u>
	☐ **Limited Treatment.** In addition to care described in Comfort Measures Only, use medical treatment, antibiotics, IV fluids and cardiac monitor as indicated. No intubation, advanced airways interventions, or mechanical ventilation. May consider less invasive airway support (e.g. CPAP, BiPAP). ***Transfer to hospital, if indicated. Avoid ICU if possible.*** <u>**Treatment Plan: Provide basic medical treatments.**</u>
	☐ **Comfort Measures Only.** Keep clean, warm and dry. Provide treatments to relieve pain and suffering through the use of any medication by any route, positioning, wound care and other measures. Use oxygen, suction and manual treatment of airway obstruction as needed for comfort. ***Patient prefers no transfer to hospital for life-sustaining treatments. Transfer if comfort needs cannot be met in current location.*** <u>**Treatment Plan: Provide treatments for comfort through symptom management.**</u>
	Additional Orders:

Section C *Check One Box Only*	**ANTIBIOTICS**
	☐ Use antibiotics if life can be prolonged. ☐ Determine use or limitation of antibiotics when infection occurs. ☐ No antibiotics except for relief of pain and discomfort.
	Additional Orders:

Section D *Check One Box in Each Column*	**ARTIFICIALLY ADMINISTERED NUTRITION AND FLUIDS: Offer food and fluids by mouth if feasible.**	
	☐ Long-term artificial nutrition by tube. ☐ Trial period of artificial nutrition by tube. ☐ Do not insert feeding tube. ☐ Decide when/if the situation arises.	☐ Long-term IV fluids. ☐ Trial period of IV fluids. ☐ No IV fluids. ☐ Decide when/if the situation arises.
	Additional Orders:	**Additional Orders:**

Section E *Signature of Physician, APRN, or PA*	**Signature of Physician, Advanced Practice Registered Nurse, or Physician Assistant** My signature below indicates to the best of my knowledge that the patient has been diagnosed with a serious illness or, based upon a medical diagnosis, may be expected to lose capacity within 12 months, and that these orders are consistent with the patient's medical condition, diagnosis, and preferences.	
Physician/APRN/PA Signature: *(required)*	Physician/APRN/PA Name: *(print)*	☐ Physician ☐ APRN ☐ PA *(Select one)*
Date: (MM/DD/YYYY) *(required)*	Physician/APRN/PA Phone Number:	Physician/APRN/PA License #:

Check everyone who participated in discussion: ☐ Patient with decision-making capacity ☐ Legal Representative ☐ Other:

Section F *Signature of Patient or Legal Representative*	**Signature of Patient or Legal Representative** I am aware that this form is voluntary. I agree that adequate information has been provided and significant thought has been given to life-prolonging measures. Treatment preferences have been expressed to the physician, physician assistant, or advanced practice registered nurse and this document reflects those treatment preferences. *If signed by a legal representative, preferences expressed must reflect patient's wishes as best understood by the legal representative.*	
Signature: *(required)*		Relationship: *(write "self" if patient)*
Print Name:	Date: (MM/DD/YYYY) *(required)*	Phone Number:

Section G *Facilitator (if applicable)*	**Facilitator Assisting with POST Form Completion (if applicable)**		
	Print Name:	Date: (MM/DD/YYYY)	Phone Number:

FORM MUST ACCOMPANY PATIENT WHEN TRANSFERRED OR DISCHARGED

POST Form	****ATTACH to Page 1****	
Patient Full Name:		

Form Completion Information (Optional but Helpful)	
Reviewed patient's advance directive to confirm no conflict with POST form: (A POST form does not replace an advance directive such as a Health Care Power of Attorney or living will.)	☐ Yes; date of the document reviewed: _____ ☐ Conflict exists, notified patient (if patient lacks capacity, noted in chart) ☐ Advance directive not available ☐ No advance directive exists

- A POST form is a designated document designed for use as part of advance care planning, the use of which must be limited to situations where the patient has been diagnosed with a serious illness or, based upon medical diagnosis, may be expected to lose capacity within 12 months and consists of a set of medical orders signed by a patient's physician, APRN, or PA addressing key medical decisions consistent with patient goals of care concerning treatment at the end of life that is portable and valid across health care settings.

- A POST form executed in South Carolina as provided in the POST Act, or a similar form executed in another jurisdiction in compliance with the laws of that jurisdiction, must be deemed a valid expression of a patient's wishes as to health care. A South Carolina health care provider or health care facility may accept a properly executed POST form as a valid expression of whether the patient consents to the provision of health care in accordance with Section 44-66-10, et seq. of the South Carolina Adult Health Care Consent Act.

- The effective date of the form is the date the POST form has been completed, executed, and signed by the Physician/APRN/PA and the patient or the patient's legal representative.

- A copy, facsimile, or electronic version of a completed POST form is considered to be legal.

- **The execution of a POST form is always voluntary and is for a person with an advanced illness.** The POST form records a patient's wishes for medical treatment in the patient's current state of health. Preferred medical treatment as stated by the patient on the POST form may be changed at any time by the patient or a designated health care representative or health care agent of the patient to reflect the patient's new wishes in accordance with the POST Act.

- Any physician who is responsible for the creation and execution of a POST form shall make reasonable efforts to periodically review and update the POST form with the patient as the patient's needs dictate but at least once per year.

- A patient's legal representative is defined under the POST Act to mean a person with priority to make health care decisions for patient pursuant to Section 44-66-10, et seq. of the South Carolina Adult Health Care Consent Act.

- An APRN may create, execute and sign a POST form if authorized to do so by his or her practice agreement. The POST form must be for a patient of the APRN, the physician with whom the APRN has entered into a practice agreement, or both.

- A PA may create, execute, and sign a POST form if authorized to do so by his or her scope of practice guidelines. The POST form must be for a patient of that PA, the PA's supervising physician, or both.

Revocation of POST Form

- A POST form may be revoked at any time by an oral or written statement by the patient or a patient's legal representative.

- A revocation is only effective upon communication to the health care provider or health care facility by the patient or the patient's legal representative.

- The execution of a POST form by a patient, or the patient's legal representative, pursuant to the POST Act, automatically revokes any previously executed POST form.

- A POST form executed pursuant to the POST Act remains effective until revoked or until a new POST form is executed pursuant to the POST Act.

Nothing herein shall be construed as legal advice.

FORM MUST ACCOMPANY PATIENT WHEN TRANSFERRED OR DISCHARGED

CHAPTER 14
FORM 8: DURABLE POWER OF ATTORNEY

FORM LETS POWER BE GIVEN OVER PROPERTY, MONEY, AND MORE

This form lets person give power to someone they name to do things. The form is called "durable" which means it is valid even if a person is later incapacitated, but the form has no power after a person's death.

FORM GIVES POWER TO LET SOMEONE CONTROL PROPERTY AND MONEY

Form lets person give power to someone to do actions involving their money, property, or other things. In form the person giving power is called "Principal" and person getting power called "Agent" (sometimes called an "Attorney-in-Fact") who is often a spouse, relative, or friend. This lets someone help do things like pay bills, use accounts, buy or sell items, sign contracts, hire workers, take out debt, and get records. The form may help if person is sick or busy, and may avoid more serious legal options. A person who isn't incapacitated can overrule or fire Agent so really power is shared. Naming a 2nd person to serve if needed is rarely needed so often skipped. If Agent signs things they should write they're using a Power of Attorney.

USING FORM CAN BE RISKY AND POWERS MAY NOT COVER UNUSUAL ACTS

Doing this form can be risky since an Agent can waste money, invest badly, or steal. There is a duty to act reasonably and Agents can be sued later, but they may be out of money. Banks or others often can't be blamed for obeying an Agent. Many people skip this form as too risky. Importantly, state law says certain big powers are not given unless a document specifically lists a power, and this book's form only lists more common powers. This means less common things maybe can't be done by Agent with Principal's things, like a) make big gifts to family, friends, and themselves, b) do unusual investments, or c) give to charity. It is better if a person if they can directly does unusual things not an Agent. Many people skip this form.

POWER OVER MINOR CHILD MAY BE GIVEN IN FORM

Usually a Power of Attorney document can give any power, and many states' laws say this lets parent in a form give power over child under 18 to let person help with child if needed (like if both parents aren't near). Some states have forms for this, like North Carolina's "Authorization To Consent To Health Care For Minor". South Carolina law doesn't specify it this is allowed and local judges prefer a parent at court name guardian if it seems needed, like due to bad illness, work far away, or military deployment. But some South Carolina lawyers do use a Power of Attorney form that says it can give power over a child, and this book's form has this option for parents with young child to choose. Frankly, rarely do children cause legal problems since a parent by cell phone can talk and approve things like with a school, doctors will give health care that safety requires, and in South Carolina a child at 16 can authorize most treatments themselves except full surgery.

PERSON SIGNS FORM IN FRONT OF 2 WITNESSES AND NOTARY

The form must be signed by person doing form in front of 2 witnesses who then sign all in front of a notary who then notarizes the form. A witness can't be a person named Agent in the form. To cancel form a person should take back copies and usually tell places shown the form. At end of form is a "Certification" an Agent can later sign if a bank or other party asks for proof the Power of Attorney is still valid.

SOUTH CAROLINA
DURABLE POWER OF ATTORNEY

APPOINTMENT OF AGENT

I, _____ (Principal's name) who reside at
_____ (Principal's address), have
this day appointed _____ (Agent's name) who resides at
_____ (Agent's address) to serve as
my Agent (called hereinafter "Agent") and to exercise the powers set forth below.

DURABILITY

This legal document shall not be affected by physical disability or mental incompetence of the Principal which renders them incapable of managing their own estate, and this is a Durable Power of Attorney.

POWERS

I give my Agent full power, authority, and discretion involving my property of any kind, money, right, or any other thing of mine or involving me, and they may do any action and make any decision I could do if I were personally present and acting. I understand this grant of power may be otherwise limited by South Carolina law but to the extent allowed this is a General Power of Attorney.

Power and authorization given by the document <u>includes but is not limited to the following</u>:

(1) to sell any and every kind of property that I may own now or in the future, real and personal, tangible, intangible and/or mixed, including without being limited to real estate, stocks, bonds, interests in partnerships, limited liability companies and any other securities, contingent and expectant interests, marital rights and any rights of survivorship incident to joint tenancy or tenancy by the entirety, upon such terms and conditions and security as my Agent shall deem appropriate and to grant options with respect to sales thereof; including to make such disposition of the proceeds of such sale or sales (including expending such proceeds for my benefit) as my Agent shall deem appropriate;

(2) to buy every kind of property, real, or personal, tangible, intangible or mixed, including, without limitation, real estate, stocks, bonds, interests in partnerships, limited liability companies and any other securities upon such terms and conditions as my Agent shall deem appropriate; to obtain options with respect to such purchases; to arrange for appropriate disposition, use, safekeeping and/or insuring of any such property purchased by my Agent; (a) to use any credit card held in my name to make such purchases and to sign any charge slips as may be necessary to use credit cards; (b) to repay from any funds belonging to me any money borrowed and to pay for any purchases made or cash advanced using credit cards issued to me;

(3) to invest and reinvest all or any part of my property in any property or interests of any kind in property, real or personal, tangible, intangible or mixed, wherever located, including without being limited to securities of all kinds, interests in limited partnerships or limited liability companies, real estate or any interest in real estate whether or not productive at the time of investment, interests in trusts, or annuity contracts without being limited by any statute or rule of law concerning investments by fiduciaries; to sell (including short sales) and end investments whether made by me or my Agent; to establish, use and terminate savings and money market accounts with financial institutions of all kinds;

(4) with respect to real property (including but not limited to any real property described on any exhibit attached to this instrument and any real property I may hereafter acquire or receive and my personal residence); to lease, sublease, release; to eject, remove and relieve tenants or other persons from, and recover possession of by all lawful means; to accept real property as gift or as security for a loan; to collect, sue for, receive and receipt for rents and profits and to conserve, invest or utilize any and all of such rents, profits and receipts to do any act of management and conservation, to pay, compromise, or to contest tax assessments and to apply for refunds in connections therewith; to vote, or give proxies to vote, with or without the power of substitution at homeowners association meetings; to hire assistance and labor; to subdivide, develop, dedicate to public use without consideration, and/or dedicate easements over; to maintain, protect, repair, preserve, insure, build upon, demolish, alter or improve all or any part thereof; to obtain or vacate plats and adjust boundaries; to adjust differences in valuation on exchange or partition by giving or receiving consideration; to release or partially release real property from a lien;

(5) with respect to personal property; to lease, sublease, and release; to recover possession of by all lawful means; to collect, sue for, receive and receipt for rents and profits therefrom; to maintain, protect, repair, preserve, insure, alter or improve all or any part thereof;

(6) to continue the operation of any business including, but not limited to, a ranch or farm, sole proprietorship, partnership, limited liability company or corporation belonging to me or in which I have a substantial interest, for such time and in such manner as my Agent shall deem appropriate, including but not limited to hiring and discharging my employees, employing legal, accounting, financial and other consultants; executing business tax returns and other government forms required to be filed by my business, paying all business related expenses, transacting all kinds of business for me in my name and on my behalf, contributing additional capital to the business, changing the name and/or the form of the business, incorporating the business, entering into such partnership agreement or limited liability company with other persons as my Agent shall deem appropriate, joining in any plan of reorganization, consolidation or merger of such business, selling, liquidating or closing out such business at such time an upon such terms as my Agent shall deem appropriate and representing me in establishing the value of any business under "Buy-Out" or "Buy-Sell" agreements to which I may be a party; to create, continue or terminate retirement plans with respect to such business and to make contributions which may be required by such plans; to borrow and pledge business assets;

(7) to exercise any right, power, privilege, or option which I may have or may claim under any contract of partnership or limited liability company or corporation, whether as a general, special or limited partner or member or shareholder; to modify or terminate my interest upon such terms and conditions as my Agent may deem appropriate; to enforce the terms of any such partnership agreement, limited liability company agreement or corporate by-laws for my protection, whether by action, proceeding or otherwise as my agent shall deem appropriate; to defend, submit to arbitration, settle or compromise any action or other legal proceeding to which I am a party because of my membership in such partnership, limited liability company or corporation;

(8) to establish accounts of all kinds, including checking and savings, for me with financial institutions of any kind, including but not limited to banks and thrift institutions, to modify, terminate, make deposits to and write checks on or make withdrawals from and grant security interests in all accounts in my name or with respect to which I am an authorized signatory (except accounts held by me in a fiduciary capacity), whether or not any such account was established by me or for me by my Agent, to negotiate, endorse, or transfer any checks or other instruments with respect to any such accounts; to contract for any services rendered by any bank or financial institution;

(9) to contract with any institution for the maintenance of a safe deposit box in my name; to have

access to all safe deposit boxes in my name or with respect to which I am an authorized signatory, whether or not the contract for such safe deposit box was executed by me (either alone or jointly with others) or by my Agent in my name; to add to and remove from the contents of any such safe deposit box and to terminate any and all contracts for such boxes; to have access at any time or times to any safe deposit box rented by me, wherever located, in order to remove any document; and any institution where a safe deposit box is located is not required to make any inquiry, and shall not incur liability to me or my estate as a result of permitting my Agent in any legal document to use this power. This power is exercisable without: (a) any contact with or notice to me, my spouse, or interested persons to my estate; (b) any prior court order or authorization; (c) any knowledge of or any prior determination as to my mental or physical capacity or incapacity; (d) any knowledge as to my whereabouts regardless whether my whereabouts are known or unknown; or (e) any other inquiry;

(10) to institute, supervise, prosecute, defend, intervene in, abandon, compromise, arbitrate, settle, dismiss, and appeal from any and all legal, equitable, judicial, or administrative hearings, actions, suits, proceedings, attachments, arrests, or distresses, involving me in any way, including but not limited to claims by or against me arising out of property damages or personal injuries suffered by or caused by me or under such circumstances that the loss resulting therefrom will or may become my responsibility and otherwise to engage in litigation involving me, my property or any interest of mine, including any property or interest or person for which or whom I have or may have any responsibility;

(11) to borrow money for my use upon such terms and conditions as my Agent shall deem appropriate and to secure such borrowing by the granting of security interests in any property or interest in property which I may now or hereafter own; to borrow money upon any life insurance policies owned by me upon my life and to grant a security interest in such policy to secure any such loans; and no insurance company shall be under any obligation whatsoever to determine the need for such loan or the application of the proceeds by my Agent;

(12) to execute a revocable trust agreement with such trustee or trustees as my Agent shall select, which trust shall provide that all income and principal shall be paid to me or to some person for my benefit, or applied for my benefit in such amounts as I or my Agent shall request or as the trustee or trustees shall determine. On my death any remaining income and principal which are assets of the revocable trust shall be paid to my personal representative and the trust shall end. The revocable trust may be revoked or amended by me or my Agent at any time and from time to time; provided, however, that any amendment by my Agent must be such that by law or under the provisions of this instrument, such amendment could have been included in the original trust agreement or if amended by me, that I have the capacity to amend the trust. My Agent may also deliver and convey any or all of my assets to the trustee or trustees thereof; add any or all of my assets to such a trust already in existence at time of creation of this instrument or created by me at any time thereafter, and for the purpose of funding any trust, to enter and remove any of my cash or property from any safe deposit box of mine (whether the box is registered in my name alone or jointly with one or more persons);

(13) to represent me in all tax matters; to prepare, sign, and file federal, state, and/or local income, gift and other tax returns of all kinds, and any and all other tax related documents; to pay taxes due, collect and make such disposition of refunds as my Agent shall deem appropriate; to post bonds, receive confidential information, and contest deficiencies determined by the Internal Revenue Service and/or any state and/or local taxing authority; to exercise any elections I may have under federal, state, or local tax law; and generally to represent me or obtain professional representation for me in all tax matters and proceedings of all kinds and for all periods before all officers of the Internal Revenue Service and state and local authorities; to engage, compensate and discharge attorneys, accountants and other tax and financial advisers and consultants who represent and/or assist me in

connection with any and all tax matters involving or in any way related to me or any property in which I have or may have any interest or responsibility;

(14) to support and/or continue to support any person whom I have undertaken to support or to whom I may owe an obligation of support, in the same manner and in accordance with the same standard of living as I may have provided in the past (adjusted if necessary by circumstances and inflation), including but not limited to the payment of real property taxes, payments on loans secured by my residence, maintenance of my residence, making payments for food, clothing and shelter, medical care, normal vacations, travel expenses, and education;

(15) to renounce any fiduciary position to which I have been or may be appointed or elected, including but not limited to personal representative, trustee, guardian, attorney-in-fact, officer or director of a corporation; and any governmental or political office or position to which I have been or may by elected or appointed; to resign any such positions in which capacity I am presently serving; to file an accounting with a court of competent jurisdiction or settle the accounting on a receipt and release or such other informal method as my Agent shall deem appropriate;

(16) to lend money and property at such interest, terms and conditions, and security my Agent deems appropriate; to renew, extend, and modify any such loan or loans that I may have previously made;

(17) to purchase, maintain, surrender, collect, or cancel (a) life insurance or annuities of any kind on my life or on the life of anyone for whom I have an insurable interest, (b) liability insurance protecting me and my estate against third party claims, (c) hospital insurance, medical insurance, Medicare supplement insurance, prescription drug insurance, dental insurance, vision insurance, custodial care insurance, and disability income insurance for me or any of my dependents, and (d) casualty insurance insuring assets of mine against loss or damage due to fire, theft, or other commonly insured risk; to pay all insurance premiums, to select any options under such policies; to increase coverage under any such policy; to borrow against any such policy; to pursue all insurance claims on my behalf; to adjust insurance losses; to apply the foregoing powers to private and public plans, including but not limited to Medicare, Medicaid, SSI and Worker's Compensation; to designate and change beneficiaries of insurance policies insuring my life and beneficiaries under any annuity contract I have an interest in; to decrease coverage under or cancel any of the policies described herein; to receive and make such disposition of the cash value upon termination of any such policy as my Agent shall deem appropriate;

(18) to renounce and disclaim any property or interest in property or powers to which for any reason and by any means I may become entitled, whether by gift, testate or intestate succession; to release or abandon any property or interest in property or powers which I may now or hereafter own,[including any interests in or rights over trusts (including the right to alter, amend, revoke or terminate)] and to exercise any right to claim an elective share in any estate or under any will. In exercising such discretion, my Agent may take into account such matters as shall include, but shall not be limited to any reduction in estate or inheritance taxes on my estate, and the effect of such renunciation or disclaimer upon persons interested in my estate and persons who would receive the renounced or disclaimed property; provided, however, that my Agent shall make no disclaimer that is expressly prohibited by other provisions of this instrument;

(19) to access and control all digital information and digital assets of mine, including but not limited to: (a) any electronically stored information of mine; (b) the contents of any electronic communications; (c) any digital asset; (d) any user account; (e) any electronic device; (f) any data storage or medium; and (g) any similar assets that may exist as technology develops;

(20) to exercise all the powers and authority granted in South Carolina Code Sections 62-8-204 through 62-8-216, as amended, except as otherwise provided in this document.

GIFTS

My Agent has the authority to make gifts, grants, or other transfers without consideration either outright or in trust, (including the forgiveness of indebtedness and the completion of any charitable pledges I may have made) to such person or organizations as my Agent shall select; to make payments for the college and post-graduate tuition and medical care of my spouse and dependents; to consent to the splitting of gifts under Sections 2513 of the Internal Revenue Code and any successor sections thereto and/or similar provisions of any state or local gift tax laws; to pay any gift tax that may arise by reason of such gift; provided, however, that my Agent and any donee of a gift shall be responsible as equity and justice may require to the extent that a gift made by my Agent is inconsistent with prudent estate planning or financial management principles or with my known or probable intent with respect to the disposition of my estate.

CARE AND CONTROL OF MY PERSON

My Agent is authorized: To do all acts necessary for maintaining my customary standard of living, to provide living quarters by purchase, lease or other arrangement, or by payment of the operating costs of my existing living quarters, including interest, amortization payments, repairs and taxes, to provide normal domestic help for the operation of my household, to provide clothing, transportation, medicine, food and incidentals, and if necessary to make all necessary arrangements, contractual or otherwise, for me at any hospital, hospice, nursing home, convalescent home, or similar place.

POWER OVER MINOR CHILD

[   ]   By initialing this box I hereby give the above-named Agent full power and authority to take any action and make any decision involving a minor child of whom I am a parent and have custody of with the following names and dates of birth:

_____ born on _____

_____ born on _____

This Agent may do anything that I could if I were present involving such a child and has full power and authority over the care, custody, rights, property, money, school, home, discipline, and insurance and benefits any such minor child, however no power over marriage or adoption is given.

Power over health care of the child is given and Agent may do anything which may be necessary, proper, or helpful to provide for the health care of the minor child, including, but not limited to:

(a) to provide for such health care at any hospital or other institution, or the employing of any physician, dentist, nurse, or other person whose services may be needed for such health care,

(b) to consent to and authorize any health care, including administration of anesthesia, X-ray examination, performance of operations, and other procedures by physicians, dentists, and other medical personnel except the withholding or withdrawal of life sustaining procedures,

(c) move and authorize admission of children to any hospital, clinic, or other facility of any kind that provides care or testing, and

(d) access and obtain all records, information, and other documents involving the health of the child and speak to and get information from all health care personnel.

OPTIONAL INSTRUCTIONS

I am not required to but I do hereby give my above-named Agent the following instructions:

_____
_____
_____
_____
_____
_____
_____
_____
_____
_____
_____
_____
_____
_____
_____
_____
_____
_____
_____
_____

ADMINISTRATIVE PROVISIONS

The following provisions shall apply to this Power of Attorney:

(1) To the extent that I am permitted by law to do so, I herewith nominate, constitute, and appoint my Agent to serve as my guardian or conservator and/or in any similar representative capacity, and if I am not permitted by law to so nominate, constitute, and appoint, then I request in the strongest possible terms that any court of competent jurisdiction which may receive and be asked to act upon a petition by any person to appoint a guardian, conservator, or similar representative for me give the greatest possible weight to this request.

(2) If any part of any provision of this instrument shall be invalid or unenforceable under applicable law, such part shall be ineffective to the extent of such invalidity only, without in any way affecting the remaining parts of such provision or the remaining provision of this instrument unless retaining the remaining provisions would be contrary to the purposes of this instrument.

(3) This instrument shall be governed by the laws of South Carolina in all respects, including its validity, construction, interpretation and termination, and to the extent permitted by law shall be applicable to all property of mine, real or personal, tangible, intangible or mixed, wherever and in whatever state of the United States or foreign country the situs of such property is at any time located and whether such property is now owned by me or hereafter acquired by me or for me by my Agent.

(4) Whenever one of the following words appears in this Power of Attorney, the word shall have the meaning set forth below: (a) "Agent" or any modifying or equivalent word or substituted pronoun

therefor is used in this instrument, such word or words shall be held and taken to include both the singular and the plural, the masculine, feminine and neuter gender thereof; and (b) "Guardian" or "Conservator" or any modifying or equivalent word or substituted pronoun is used in this instrument, such word or words shall be held and taken to mean respectively the fiduciary (appointed by a court of competent jurisdiction or by other lawful means) responsible for person and/or the property of an individual.

(5) This instrument may be amended or revoked by me, and my Agent and any successor agent may be removed by me at any time by the execution by me of a written instrument of revocation, amendment, or removal delivered to my Agent and to all successor agents. If this instrument has been recorded in the public records, then the instrument of revocation, amendment or removal shall be filed or recorded in the same public records.

(6) My Agent and any successor agent may resign or refuse to act by informing me and any person who is acting as guardian, conservator, or trustee for me.

(7) My Agent is entitled to reimbursement for expenses paid for me and reasonable compensation.

(8) Agent may make photocopies of this instrument as frequently and in such quantity as my Agent shall deem appropriate. All photocopies shall have the same force and effect as an original.

THIRD PARTY RELIANCE

For the purpose of inducing all persons, organizations, corporations, and entities including but not limited to any physician, hospital, bank, broker, custodian, insurer, lender, transfer agent, taxing authority, governmental agency, or any other third party to act in accordance with the instructions of my Agent given in this instrument, I hereby represent, warrant and agree that:

(1) If this instrument is revoked or amended for any reason, I, my estate, my heirs, successors, and assigns will hold any person, organization, corporation, or entity (hereinafter referred to in the aggregate as "Person") harmless from any loss suffered, or liability incurred by such Person in acting in accordance with the instructions of my Agent acting under this instrument prior to the receipt by such Person of actual knowledge of any such revocation or amendment.

(2) No person who may act in reliance upon the representations of my Agent for the scope of authority granted to the Agent shall incur any liability as to me or to my estate as a result of permitting the Agent to exercise this authority, nor is any such person who deals with my Agent responsible to determine or ensure the proper application of funds or property.

(3) The powers conferred on my agent by this instrument may be exercised by my Agent alone and my Agent's signature or act under the authority granted in this instrument may be accepted by Persons as fully authorized by me and with the same force and effect as if I were personally present, competent, and acting on my own behalf. Consequently, all acts lawfully done by my Agent hereunder are done with my consent and shall have the same validity and effect as if I were personally present and personally exercised the powers myself, and shall inure to the benefit of and bind me and my heirs, assigns and personal representatives.

(4) All Persons from whom my Agent may request information regarding me, my personal or financial affairs or any information which I am entitled to receive are hereby authorized to give such information to my Agent without limitation and are released from any legal liability whatsoever to me, my estate, my heirs and assigns for complying with my Agent's requests.

SIGNING AND NOTARY

Principal:

I, _____, the Principal, sign my name to this Power of Attorney document this day of __ day of _____, 20__, and , being first duly sworn, do declare to the undersigned authority that I sign and execute this instrument as my Power of Attorney and that I sign it willingly, or willingly direct another to sign for me, that I execute it as my free and voluntary act for the purposes expressed in the Power of Attorney and that I am 18 years of age or older, of sound mind and under no constraint or undue influence.

_____
Principal's Signature

Witnesses:

We, _____ and _____, the Witnesses who are signing our name immediately below to the foregoing Power of Attorney document being first duly sworn now do say and declare the Principal signed, sealed, published and declared this document as and for their Power of Attorney in our presence, and that we Witnesses in the presence of the Principal and each other sign this document as Witnesses to the Principal's signing and declare that to the best of our knowledge the Principal is 18 years of age or old, of sound mind, and under no constraint or undue influence.

_____   _____
Witness Signature   Witness Address

_____   _____
Witness Signature   Witness Address

Notary:

STATE OF SOUTH CAROLINA   )
)
COUNTY OF _____)

Sworn and acknowledged before me by _____ (Principal), and subscribed and sworn to before me by _____ and _____ (Witnesses), on this __ day of _____, 20__.

Signature of Notary: _____
My commission expires: _____

AGENT'S CERTIFICATION AS TO THE VALIDITY OF POWER OF ATTORNEY AND AGENT'S AUTHORITY

(optional to do anytime after the time the Power of Attorney is signed)

State of South Carolina)
)
County of _____)

I, _____ (Name of Agent), say and certify under penalty of perjury that _____(Name of Principal) granted me authority as an agent or successor agent in a Power of Attorney document dated _____.

I further say and certify that to my knowledge:

(1) the Principal is alive and has not revoked the Power of Attorney or my authority to act under the Power of Attorney and the Power of Attorney and my authority to act under the Power of Attorney have not terminated;

(2) the action I desire to take is within the scope of my authority granted under the Power of Attorney.

(3) if the Power of Attorney was drafted to become effective upon the happening of an event or contingency, the event or contingency has occurred;

(4) if I was named as a successor agent, the prior agent is no longer able or willing to serve; and

(5) Optional: _____
_____
_____.

SIGNATURE AND ACKNOWLEDGMENT:

Agent's Signature:_____   Date:_____
Agent's Printed Name:_____
Agent's Address:_____

NOTARY:

This document was acknowledged before me on _____ (date), by
_____ (Agent).

Signature of Notary: _____
My commission expires: _____

CHAPTER 15
FORM 9: FINAL WISHES

LETS PERSON BE NAMED AND INSTRUCTIONS GIVEN TO CONTROL DEAD BODY

This form lets someone be named and instructions given to control a person's body after death (their "bodily remains") and related things like funeral, burial, cremation, ceremonies, and buying things for all this.

CAN NAME PERSON TO CONTROL DEAD BODY AND GIVE INSTRUCTIONS

The form lets person give power to someone to control the dead body and related issues like funeral, burial, cremation, ceremonies, and buying goods and services for all this. If this form is not done by law control is by closest family (spouse, children, parents, then brothers or sisters).   People do this form rarely usually if it seems family may be too upset while mourning, be bad with money, or do unwanted things. Payment for things comes from pre-paid funeral accounts, insurance, and a dead person's or estate's money and property, and Executor and family legally must help arrange payment using these things. Also, the form has an area for instructions but many people skip this and trust the person named or family to do what deceased person mentioned they wanted. Legally people including family should do the funeral, burial, and related things the deceased wanted if decedent's properly, money, and estate can afford it.

MOST PEOPLE CONTROL THINGS IN HEALTH CARE POWER OF ATTORNEY

Instead of this Chapter's separate form most people who want to control this area do it in a Health Care Power Of Attorney form. In this form people can say a thing like, "My Health Care Agent shall be in charge of my bodily remains, funeral, burial, ceremonies, and related things, and do as follows:_____".

SEVERAL OPTIONS ABOUT BODILY REMAINS AND EVENTS EXIST

After a death police are told and funeral home or crematorium come get body. Half of people pick burial and half cremation. If picking cremation later "cremains" go to family or "columbarium" vault in cemetery.

Half of people do not do early events in first month when shocked family may be unready for visitors. Importantly, if "Direct Burial" or "Direct Cremation" is requested costs may be 80% off usual $10,000+ but this skips events with body till burial or cremation in done with no family involvement. Weeks later people may do ash scattering, ceremony, or dinner at park, house, church, or hall, often with food, speech, or video.

Half of people do early events within month, and there are several different options to pick from. First, some people do within days a "Vigil", "Viewing", or "Wake", where family and friends talk or just pray maybe in room with body (closed or open casket) or cremated ashes, often at Funeral Home or church. Second, some people do big ceremony within week of either a) funeral (maybe with Mass) in church with priest or minister, or b) informal event like "Celebration of Life" or "Remembrance" with or without the body. Third, some people do final event at cemetery (religious or not), like a burial or putting ashes in a vault.

SIGN FORM WITH NOTARY

To complete form it is signed by person in front of a notary who then notarizes it. Once done the form should be given to someone to hold or put in a place it can be found quickly within days of a death.

FINAL WISHES

I, _____ (name of person doing this document) as allowed by South Carolina law do order the following be done involving my dead body and all related things like funeral, burial, cremation, ceremonies, tombstone or marker, and related goods and services.

DESIGNATION OF PERSON

I designate this person to have the right to control my dead body and all related things (name and contact information for this person):

_____

INSTRUCTIONS

I want the following things involving my dead body and all related things like funeral, cremation, burial, ceremonies, tombstone or marker, and related goods and services.

_____

_____

_____

_____

_____

_____

_____

_____

_____

_____

_____

_____

_____

Signed:_____   Date:_____

STATE OF SOUTH CAROLINA   )
COUNTY OF _____   )

Sworn and acknowledged before me by _____ on this ___ day of _____, 20___.

Signature of Notary: _____

My commission expires: _____

APPENDIX: SAMPLE FILLED OUT FORMS

TO GET FORMS TO USE PEOPLE CAN:

    (1) PHOTOCOPY BOOK PAGES,

    (2) TEAR OUT PAGES FROM A BOOK, OR

    (3) DOWNLOAD BOOK WITH FORMS FROM WWW.DAVENPORTPUBLISHING.COM

AND USUALLY PDF FORM AT IS BEST TO AVOID SPACING/FORMAT CHANGES.

EMAIL ANY COMMENTS TO DAVENPORTPRESS@GMAIL.COM .

On the next pages to show how it can be done are some sample filled out legal forms.

People can add words to legal forms by computer or typewriter to be neater, but many people just by hand use pen, marker, or pencil to handwrite words into forms.

It is not required but is bit better if signatures are in ink or marker not pencil.

Many parts of the forms especially Will gifts can be left empty and unfilled.

Anyone can fill in words in legal form not just the person doing the form, like a friend with neat writing can fill in all the words, addresses, and dates that are needed. Only the final signatures must be done by each person who wants the form.

To add words in form by pen, pencil, typewriter, or computer any of these is fine:

        "I appoint _____*John Doe*_____ as Agent" ,

        "I appoint _____John Doe_____ as Agent",

        "I appoint John Doe as Agent".

When doing forms it may help to know "respectively" means "in order just stated".

People need not worry about neatness or small mistakes, and a document is usually fine if those people who knew a decedent in life can tell the likely meaning.

LAST WILL AND TESTAMENT

I, _Paul Thomas Maxwell_ , of _Greenville_ County, South Carolina, do revoke all prior Wills, Testaments, and Codicils, and do voluntarily make, publish, and declare this to be my Will. I am of sound mind and under no duress or undue influence.

1. GIFTS. I give these gifts in this Will, but to get a gift in this section the recipient must survive me except as otherwise stated below.

I give _____ to _____.

I give _____ to _____.

I give _____ to _____.

I give _____ to _____.

I give _____ to _____.

I give _____ to _____.

I give _____ to _____.

I give _____ to _____.

I give _____ to _____.

I give _____ to _____.

SKIPPED

2. GIFTS OF TANGIBLE PERSONAL PROPERTY BY SEPARATE WRITINGS. I may gift tangible personal property by writings separate from a Will. Such a writing not found within 90 days of my death is canceled and of no effect. Such a writing existing when this Will is done is not revoked or canceled unless this Will specifically says this.

3. RESIDUE. I give the rest and residue and remainder of my estate, my money and property of any kind and nature, and anything I have an interest in so long as it was not transferred by other Will provisions (all of which is called the "residue"), as follows:

a) to _Susan Lee Maxwell_ who survive me with persons just named who survive me taking the share of non-survivors, then

b) to _Oscar David Maxwell and Jennifer Judy Tabor_ and if any of those just named do not survive me their part goes to their lineal descendants, per stirpes.

4. ADMINISTRATION. I name and appoint ___*Susan Lee Maxwell*___ as Personal Representative including for me, my Will, and my estate.

5. MISCELLANEOUS. The following applies to this Will and generally.

Priority of Will gifts of the same type is based on the order they are written.

In this document no unfilled part is a mistake and residue spaces may be left blank.

The words "give" and "gift" also means a devise, bequest, grant, legacy, or similar.

A gift of property no longer owned by Testator at death shall lapse and be of no effect including no payment of money shall be done in its place, all without ademption.

If gift or gift section mentions survival, survive, or surviving then survival is an absolute condition and anti-lapse laws or similar have no effect.

Any failure to make gifts to family including children is intentional and not a mistake.

No gift or transfer made during life reduces or offsets a Will gift unless during my life I expressly usually called it a "loan" or "advancement".

Use of particular gender shall include other genders, reference to singular or plural shall be interchangeable, and "they" may be singular or plural.

Unless parts of this Will specifically says otherwise a secured debt like mortgage or lien on real property or vehicles shall not be paid off, recipient of property takes it subject to liens, and no recipient who has debtor take property or get payment via use or threat of a secured debt may require a devisee, recipient, heir, or estate to pay or do anything.

I give any Personal Representative a) the fullest authority, powers, and discretion allowed by state law, b) authority to lease, sell, mortgage, convey, or retain property including real property in any such manner and time they deem helpful or proper, and c) authority to anytime pay or settle claims or debts if they in their sole discretion chooses.

Any Personal Representative shall not be required to render and file annual or other accountings with respect to property or money including in relation to my Will or estate. Any Personal Representative may act independently in all ways without supervision.

I request informal or administrative probate of my Will and estate without supervision.

If context permits the terms Personal Representative, Executor, and Administrator shall be interchangeable as if all were written, and if context permits Conservator, Guardian of the Estate, and Guardian of Property shall be interchangeable as if all were written.

The residue includes lapsed or failed gifts, insurance paid to estate, inheritances owed me, and property I had a power of appointment or testamentary disposition over.

Any Personal Representative, Executor, Guardian of any kind, Conservator, and any fiduciary under this Will or otherwise, shall qualify and serve without bond, security, surety, or similar, including despite place of residence or lack of ties to a state or country.

Conservator and Guardian of any kind should help all persons in my care who need it. This Will does not revoke a Living Will or any legal document concerning health care.

A Personal Representative using their sole discretion has power at any time to transfer money or property of a child or mine or any minor to the person named Conservator in this Will to serve as Custodian under the South Carolina Uniform Transfers to Minors Act or a similar law anywhere, to serve until minor is 18, and all without bond or any court action. If they are unable to serve the person named Personal Representative shall be Custodian.

TESTATOR

IN WITNESS WHEREOF, I, _Paul Thomas Maxwell_ , the Testator, publish, declare, and sign this instrument as my Will this _22nd_ day of _June_ , 20 _22_ , and do hereby declare that I sign and execute this instrument as my last Will and that I sign it willingly, that I execute it as my free and voluntary act for the purposes therein expressed, and that I am 18 years of age or older, of sound mind, and under no constraint or undue influence.

Paul Thomas Maxwell
Testator signature

WITNESSES

We, _Eve Mable Rogers_ and _Mary Ann Moon_ the Witnesses, sign our names to this instrument and each of us do hereby declare that the Testator willingly publishes, declares, and signs and executes this instrument as the Testator's last Will, and that each of us, in the presence and hearing of the Testator, hereby signs this Will as Witness to the Testator's signing, and that to the best of our knowledge the Testator is 18 years of age or older, of sound mind, and under no constraint or undue influence.

Eve Mable Rogers
Witness

14 2nd St., Charleston, SC 29401
Witness Address

Mary Ann Moon
Witness

14 2nd St., Chicago, IL 66018
Witness Address

LAST WILL AND TESTAMENT

I, ____Paul Brian Kent____, of __Richland__ County, South Carolina, do revoke all prior Wills, Testaments, and Codicils, and do voluntarily make, publish, and declare this to be my Will. I am of sound mind and under no duress or undue influence.

1. GIFTS. I give these gifts in this Will, but to get a gift in this section the recipient must survive me except as otherwise stated below.

I give _big oak table_ to _Anne J. Wix._

I give ___$5,000___ to ___Loretta Marsha Switt_.

I give _63 Ivy Road, Charleston, South Carolina_ to _Kenneth Victor Poppler._

I give _all land in Richland County in South Carolina_ to _Greta Olivia Fox._

I give _903 Beach Road, Miami, FL_ to _James Eric Hanson_.

I give _Bronze Roman Lamp_ to _Anne Kilby_ and _Kevin Kilby._

I give _wedding ring_ to _Ruth Jones._

I give _all jewelry not given above_ to _Kay Pidoski._

I give ___$781.35___ to _Wanda Kay Zinski_.

I give _UBank account #8980443723_ to _Joy Rundy a fishing buddy_.

I give _Wells Fargo acct ending in #8923_ to _Lawrence Deer_.

I give _1998 Ford truck_ to _John Rupert Smith_.

I give _a total of $50,000_ to _Brian Peterson, Michael Peterson, and Mary Hart_.

I give _$200_ to _Kent Food Shelf on Smith Road in Myrtle Beach, South Carolina_.

I give _all spare tires and auto parts I own_ to _Victor Perez my mechanic_.

I give ___$1000 each___ to _each of my grandchildren_.

2. GIFTS OF TANGIBLE PERSONAL PROPERTY BY SEPARATE WRITINGS. I may gift tangible personal property by writings separate from a Will. Such a writing not found within 90 days of my death is canceled and of no effect. Such a writing existing when this Will is done is not revoked or canceled unless this Will specifically says this.

3. RESIDUE. I give the rest and residue and remainder of my estate, my property of any kind and nature, and anything I have an interest in (all of which is called the "residue"), so long as any such thing was not transferred by other Will provisions, as follows:

   a) to _____ Ruth May Kent my wife _____ who survive me with persons just named who survive me taking the share of non-survivors, then

   b) to 45% to Oscar Elliot Kent my son and 45% to Karen Lisa Lundy my daughter and 10% to Pedro Juan Sanchez and if any of those just named do not survive me their part goes to their lineal descendants, per stirpes.

4. ADMINISTRATION. I name and appoint ___ Ruth May Kent _____ as Personal Representative including for me, my Will, and my estate.

5. GUARDIANS. I name and appoint Karen Lisa Fox my sister as Guardian to make decisions and have control of any minor child of mine's health and health care, education, maintenance, support, and personal care. I also name and appoint Ruth May Kent my wife as Conservator of any minor child of mine and their money, property, and estate.

6. MISCELLANEOUS. The following applies to this Will and generally.

Priority of Will gifts of the same type is based on the order they are written.

In this document no unfilled part is a mistake and residue spaces may be left blank.

The words "give" and "gift" also means a devise, bequest, grant, legacy, or similar.

A gift of property no longer owned by Testator at death shall lapse and be of no effect including no payment of money shall be done in its place, all without ademption.

If gift or gift section mentions survival, survive, or surviving then survival is an absolute condition and anti-lapse laws or similar have no effect.

Any failure to make gifts to family including children is intentional and not a mistake.

No gift or transfer made during life reduces or offsets a Will gift unless during my life I expressly usually called it a "loan" or "advancement".

Use of particular gender shall include other genders, reference to singular or plural shall be interchangeable, and "they" may be singular or plural.

Unless parts of this Will specifically says otherwise a secured debt like mortgage or lien on real property or vehicles shall not be paid off, recipient of property takes it subject to liens, and no recipient who has debtor take property or get payment via use or threat of a secured debt may require a devisee, recipient, heir, or estate to pay or do anything.

Any Personal Representative shall not be required to render and file annual or other accountings with respect to property or money including in relation to my Will or estate. Any Personal Representative may act independently in all ways without supervision.

I request informal or administrative probate of my Will and estate without supervision.

If context permits the terms Personal Representative, Executor, and Administrator shall be interchangeable as if all were written, and if context permits Conservator, Guardian of the Estate, and Guardian of Property shall be interchangeable as if all were written.

The residue includes lapsed or failed gifts, insurance paid to estate, inheritances owed me, and property I had a power of appointment or testamentary disposition over.

Any Personal Representative, Executor, Guardian of any kind, Conservator, and any fiduciary under this Will or otherwise, shall qualify and serve without bond, security, surety, or similar, including despite place of residence or lack of ties to a state or country.

Conservator and Guardian of any kind should help all persons in my care who need it.

This Will does not revoke a Living Will or any legal document concerning health care.

A Personal Representative using their sole discretion has power at any time to transfer money or property of a child or mine or any minor to the person named Conservator in this Will to serve as Custodian under the South Carolina Uniform Transfers to Minors Act or a similar law anywhere, to serve until minor is 18, and all without bond or any court action. If they are unable to serve the person named Personal Representative shall be Custodian.

TESTATOR

IN WITNESS WHEREOF, I, __Paul Brian Kent__, the Testator, publish, declare, and sign this instrument as my Will this __30th__ day of __December__, 20 __19__, and do hereby declare that I sign and execute this instrument as my last Will and that I sign it willingly, that I execute it as my free and voluntary act for the purposes therein expressed, and that I am 18 years of age or older, of sound mind, and under no constraint or undue influence.

Paul Brian Kent
Testator signature

WITNESSES

We, ___Olivia Joy Pawlenty___ and ___Roy Felix Pawlenty___, the Witnesses, sign our names to this instrument and each of us do hereby declare that the Testator willingly publishes, declares, and signs and executes this instrument as the Testator's last Will, and that each of us, in the presence and hearing of the Testator, hereby signs this Will as Witness to the Testator's signing, and that to the best of our knowledge the Testator is 18 years of age or older, of sound mind, and under no constraint or undue influence.

Olivia Joy Pawlenty	87 Hastings Avenue, Columbia, SC 29044
Witness	Address
Roy Felix Pawlenty	87 Hastings Avenue, Columbia, SC 29044
Witness	Address

LAST WILL AND TESTAMENT

I, **David Eric Smith**, of **Greenville** County, South Carolina, do revoke all prior Wills, Testaments, and Codicils, and do voluntarily make, publish, and declare this to be my Will. I am of sound mind and under no duress or undue influence.

1. GIFTS. I give these gifts in this Will, but to get a gift in this section the recipient must survive me except as otherwise stated below.

I give _____ $500 _____ to _each of my brothers, sisters, and cousins_____ .

I give _____ $1000 _____ to ____ Baker Food Shelf in Columbia, South Carolina_____ .

2. GIFTS OF TANGIBLE PERSONAL PROPERTY BY SEPARATE WRITINGS. I may gift tangible personal property by writings separate from a Will. Such a writing not found within 90 days of my death is canceled and of no effect. Such a writing existing when this Will is done is not revoked or canceled unless this Will specifically says this.

3. RESIDUE. The rest and residue and remainder of my estate, my property of any kind and nature, and anything I have an interest in, I give to **Adam Michael Smith and Ann Sue Baker who survive me** and to lineal descendants per stirpes of a person just named who did not survive me.

4. ADMINISTRATION. I name and appoint **Ann Sue Baker** as Personal Representative including for me, my Will, and my estate.

5. MISCELLANEOUS. The following applies to this Will and generally.
   Priority of Will gifts of the same type is based on the order they are written.
   In this document no unfilled part is a mistake and residue spaces may be left blank.
   The words "give" and "gift" also means a devise, bequest, grant, legacy, or similar.
   A gift of property no longer owned by Testator at death shall lapse and be of no effect including no payment of money shall be done in its place, all without ademption.
   If gift or gift section mentions survival, survive, or surviving then survival is an absolute condition and anti-lapse laws or similar have no effect.

Any failure to make gifts to family including children is intentional and not a mistake.

No gift or transfer made during life reduces or offsets a Will gift unless during my life I expressly usually called it a "loan" or "advancement".

Use of particular gender shall include other genders, reference to singular or plural shall be interchangeable, and "they" may be singular or plural.

Unless parts of this Will specifically says otherwise a secured debt like mortgage or lien on real property or vehicles shall not be paid off, recipient of property takes it subject to liens, and no recipient who has debtor take property or get payment via use or threat of a secured debt may require a devisee, recipient, heir, or estate to pay or do anything.

I give any Personal Representative a) the fullest authority, powers, and discretion allowed by state law, b) authority to lease, sell, mortgage, convey, or retain property including real property in any such manner and time they deem helpful or proper, and c) authority to anytime pay or settle claims or debts if they in their sole discretion chooses.

Any Personal Representative shall not be required to render and file annual or other accountings with respect to property or money including in relation to my Will or estate. Any Personal Representative may act independently in all ways without supervision.

I request informal or administrative probate of my Will and estate without supervision.

If context permits the terms Personal Representative, Executor, and Administrator shall be interchangeable as if all were written, and if context permits Conservator, Guardian of the Estate, and Guardian of Property shall be interchangeable as if all were written.

The residue includes lapsed or failed gifts, insurance paid to estate, inheritances owed me, and property I had a power of appointment or testamentary disposition over.

Any Personal Representative, Executor, Guardian of any kind, Conservator, and any fiduciary under this Will or otherwise, shall qualify and serve without bond, security, surety, or similar, including despite place of residence or lack of ties to a state or country.

Conservator and Guardian of any kind should help all persons in my care who need it.

This Will does not revoke a Living Will or any legal document concerning health care.

A Personal Representative using their sole discretion has power at any time to transfer money or property of a child or mine or any minor to the person named Conservator in this Will to serve as Custodian under the South Carolina Uniform Transfers to Minors Act or a similar law anywhere, to serve until minor is 18, and all without bond or any court action. If they are unable to serve the person named Personal Representative shall be Custodian.

TESTATOR

IN WITNESS WHEREOF, I, **David Eric Smith**, the Testator, publish, declare, and sign this instrument as my Will this **21st** day of **June**, 2021, and do hereby declare that I sign and execute this instrument as my last Will and that I sign it willingly, that I execute it as my free and voluntary act for the purposes therein expressed, and that I am 18 years of age or older, of sound mind, and under no constraint or undue influence.

David Eric Smith

Testator signature

WITNESSES

We, **Harriet Potter** and **Pamela Bonnie Rooker**, the Witnesses, sign our names to this instrument and each of us do hereby declare that the Testator willingly publishes, declares, and signs and executes this instrument as the Testator's last Will,

and that each of us, in the presence and hearing of the Testator, hereby signs this Will as Witness to the Testator's signing, and that to the best of our knowledge the Testator is 18 years of age or older, of sound mind, and under no constraint or undue influence.

Harriet Potter

Witness signature

204 Main Street, Buffalo, SC 29044

Witness address

Pamela Bonnie Rooker

Witness signature

83 River Road, West Charleston, SC 29054

Witness address

SELF-PROVING AFFIDAVIT

(S.C. Code § 62-2-503)

State of South Carolina

County of _Greenville_

We, _David Eric Smith_ and _Harriet Potter_ and _Pamela Bonnie Rooker_ the Testator and at least one of the Witnesses (but a second Witness can also be named here and do this form), respectively, whose names are signed to the attached or foregoing instrument, being first duly sworn, do hereby declare to the undersigned authority that

the Testator signed and executed the instrument as their last Will and that they had signed willingly, and that they executed it as their free and voluntary act for the purposes therein expressed, and

that each of the Witnesses, in the presence and hearing of the Testator, signed the Will as Witness and to the best of their knowledge the testator was at that time 18 years of age or older, of sound mind, and under no constraint or undue influence.

David Eric Smith
Testator

Harriet Potter   _Pamela Bonnie Rooker_
Witness(es)

Subscribed, sworn to, and acknowledged before me by _David Eric Smith_, the Testator, and subscribed and sworn to before me by one or more Witnesses, _Harriet Potter and Pamela Bonnie Rooker_ , this _21st_ day of _June_, 20 _21_.

Melissa Leigh Ulbin
NOTARY PUBLIC FOR SOUTH CAROLINA
My Commission Expires:_____

Melissa Leigh Ulbin
Notary Public, State of South Carolina
My Commission Expires May 15, 2025

TANGIBLE PERSONAL PROPERTY LIST

In this writing are gifts of tangible personal property to occur at my death, but this writing if not found by someone within 90 days of my death is void and canceled.

I may do many of these writings which should be seen as 1 document with the more recent writing controlling if any gifts conflict.

If a person getting a gift below does not survive me such gift is void and canceled.

PROPERTY ITEMS		NAMES OF RECIPIENTS
1998 Ford Truck	to	Samantha Bell
1.3 carat diamond ring + Irish rings	to	Ann Sue Reed
14 ft power boat + kayak + paddles	to	L. Wheeler
Amish style bench	to	Reba Stewart
glass table, telescope, umbrellas	to	Rebecca Stewart
Irish wood cups, oak platter, red vase	to	Mary and Cindy Lott
painting of sailboat in storm	to	Mary Lott
chainsaw marked with 382937	to	Mary Lott
chainsaw marked with 89930	to	Matt Smith
antique lanterns + repair kits	to	Sue Wu maid at Hart Hotel
oak lamp kept on porch	to	Mary Kay Poppler
sewing machines	to	Mary Kay Poppler
rocking chair bought in Oregon	to	Don Winkler boat mechanic
all fishing poles and fishing nets	to	Joe "Fish" Hoss, fishing pal
hats at cabin	to	Ken Baker
	to	
	to	

DATE: _2-12-2023_   SIGNED: _David Eric Smith_